Even before the Norman Conquest Norwich was one of the most important provincial centres in England. It has maintained its status through the centuries, and its history therefore is complex and fascinating. From this rich web Elsie McCutcheon has drawn an assortment of strands which are particularly appealing. Some of these deal with personalities like Margaret Paston, a redoubtable lady of the 15th century; Sir Thomas Browne, the 17th century polymath; or John Crome who founded the Norwich School of artists. Some concern important events – the visit to Norwich of Queen Elizabeth the First; the Great Flood of 1878; the riot of 1272. There are chapters on religious persecution, on 18th century philanthropy, on industrial disturbances.

The author has consulted a wide variety of sources in her researches and made use of contemporary newspapers. The result is a book which contains an attractive blend of the familiar and the less well-known. It will appeal both to the 'fine old city's' residents and to its many visitors.

Elsie McCutcheon is a native of Glasgow. She taught English there before moving to Norfolk in 1964. She lived in the village of Drayton near Norwich for fourteen years and during that period became involved in amateur archaeology and local history research. She was Publicity Officer for Norfolk Archaeology Rescue Group and wrote a thesis on St Faith's Workhouse for the Cambridge University Extra-Mural Board's Local History Certificate.

Her published works include six children's novels (five of them historical and with an East Anglian setting); an informal history of Bury St Edmunds; and numerous articles and short stories for magazines and newspapers. She now lives in Suffolk but returns frequently to Norwich.

Also by Elsie McCutcheon

Bury St Edmunds: Historic Town

for children

The Moonlight Paupers
Summer of the Zeppelin
Runner-up for the Guardian Award 1983
The Rat War
Smokescreen
Storm Bird
Twisted Truth

NORWICH THROUGH THE AGES

The Ferry, Lower Close.

NORWICH
THROUGH THE AGES

Elsie McCutcheon

The Alastair Press

Published by
The Alastair Press
2 Hatter Street
Bury St Edmunds
Suffolk

First published in 1989
© Elsie McCutcheon 1989

ISBN 1 870567 80 3 paper
ISBN 1 870567 46 3 cloth

Typeset in 11/14 Bembo by
Rowland Phototypesetting Ltd
Bury St Edmunds, Suffolk
Printed in Great Britain by
St Edmundsbury Press Ltd
Bury St Edmunds, Suffolk

Cover illustration by Sir J. Arnesby Brown, 'View of
Norwich 1934–5', by kind permission of Norfolk
Museums Service (Norwich Castle Museum). This view is
taken from the Bungay Road.

For my friend, Pat Benson, who helps to mould the 'fine citizens' of tomorrow

Contents

List of illustrations

Foreword

This book has been born of many hours of study over several years, in the Colman and Rye Library, and the Norfolk and Norwich Record Office. Thus I have to thank a succession of archivists and librarians for assistance. I must also thank the following individuals; Norma Watt of the Castle Museum for help in choosing illustrations; Stephen and Alison du Sautoy of the Alastair Press for encouraging me to write this book and patiently awaiting it: Dr Pat Murrell for historical advice and practical assistance on the home front; Peter Northeast and David Dymond for frequently providing transport to Norwich, as well as convivial company and the benefit of their expertise; Rachel Young whose lectures first gave me an appetite for Norwich history; and finally, my daughter, Alison, whose love for Norwich and her native county of Norfolk has always been an inspiration.

Elsie McCutcheon
September 1989

Lady Emma's Siege

For three months in 1075 a woman called Emma held Norwich Castle against the besieging troops of King William the First. This was no act of defiance by a female Hereward the Wake against her Norman overlord. It was the penultimate scene in a drama of power-politics, initiated by Emma's husband, Ralf de Guader, Earl of East Anglia, and her brother, Roger Fitzwilliam, Earl of Hereford. It is a story of treason and internecine strife.

Emma and Roger were the children of William Fitz-Osbern, a cousin of the Conqueror, and his close friend from boyhood. In the days when William was no more than Duke of Normandy and known as 'the Bastard' rather than 'the Conqueror', Fitz-Osbern was his Seneschal. After the Conquest he became one of the new king's viceroys in England, the other being King William's half-brother, Bishop Odo. Fitz-Osbern was renowned for his fighting prowess. In 1069 he helped to crush the rebellious Northumbrians. He also supervised the building of many of the castles which King William was hastily erecting to intimidate the native population. Among these was probably Norwich Castle, not the stone keep we see today, but a wooden construction built on top of a mound. Fitz-Osbern was King William's loyal friend and servant to the day of his death in 1071. But if William expected to find the same qualities in Fitz-Osbern's children, he was to be sorely disappointed.

Fitz-Osbern had been Earl of Hereford. Fitzwilliam inherited this title. In 1075 in blatant defiance of the King's wishes he gave his sister, Emma, in marriage to Ralf Guader, Earl of East Anglia. Earl Ralf was a Breton, who had deserted his liege-lord, King Harold Godwineson, to fight on Duke William's side in 1066. He had been rewarded with the earldom which had been Gyrth Godwineson's before the latter died at Hastings by his brother's side. In 1075 Earl Ralf was an important and powerful man holding the borough of Norwich from the King as well as many manors throughout East Anglia. It is understandable that King William should be reluctant to see an alliance between these two noblemen. From the other side of the Channel he had watched his kinsman, Edward the Confessor, struggle for years to keep in check the power of his father-in-law, Earl Godwin and his six ambitious sons. He had watched the House of Godwin swallow up earldom after earldom and place its friends in high places in the Church, dispossessing Edward's Normans. William doubtless did not want to see another powerful faction in the making.

By necessity King William was an 'absentee landlord' during much of his reign. His estates in Normandy were under constant threat from neighbouring rulers. By 1075, too, his position in England seemed secure. The Godwins had been wiped out. The various minor English uprisings had been effectively crushed. The Church and most of the country were in the hands of Norman nobles. It is not surprising then that when the marriage of Emma and Ralf Guader took place, their monarch was not in England. The 'cat' was away, and the 'mice' took advantage. A splendid wedding-feast was held at Exning, near Newmarket. One of the few remaining English earls was invited. He was Waltheof, Earl of Northumberland.

Waltheof, one of the most renowned military leaders in the country, had been no friend of the Normans. He had fought bravely with King Harold Godwineson both at Stamford Bridge and at Hastings. In 1067 he had been among the hostages taken back to Normandy by William. In 1069 having returned to his own country he had fought with the Northern rebels against the King. Despite his record, William had pardoned him and allowed him to keep his earldom. Perhaps he thought it wiser to have Waltheof as a fighting ally than as a dead folk-hero, but Earl Ralf and Roger Fizwilliam knew Waltheof's worth as an ally too. During the wedding-feast they took him aside, told him that they had plans to stage a coup in the King's absence, and invited the Northumbrian earl to join them. With Fitzwilliam's force in the west, Earl Ralf's in the east, and Waltheof's in the north, rising simultaneously, the rebellion might well have been successful.

To begin with Waltheof agreed to join the conspirators or pretended to fall in with them. He then went to Lanfranc, the Archbishop of Canterbury and the King's trusted adviser, and told him of the plot. Lanfranc wasted no time in organising his forces. When Fitzwilliam returned to Hereford to raise his standard, he found his army confronted by a body of soldiers led by Sheriff Urse of Worcestershire, by the Abbot of Evesham, and by Bishop Wulfstan of Worcester, who had been King Harold's friend and confessor. Fitzwilliam was ignominiously defeated and taken prisoner.

Earl Ralf and Emma had not travelled far from Exning when their band was opposed by a much larger body of fighting men led by the formidable Bishop Odo, Bishop Geoffrey of Coutance, and William de Warenne, Earl of Kent (and builder of Castle Acre). Routed, Earl Ralf and Emma fled to Norwich. According to the chronicles, all those who were taken prisoner, had their right feet amputated to mark them forever as traitors.

Whenever there was rebellion in England, the Scandi-
navians were always ready to lend a hand. It was only forty
years previously that King Cnut, England's Danish
monarch, had died. So it was to Denmark that Earl Ralf
looked for help. In a last desperate attempt to save himself
from ignominy and the King's retribution, he set sail for
Denmark leaving his wife to defend the garrisoned castle
until his return.

Emma and her troops managed to withstand a determined military siege for three months, but Danish assistance was not forthcoming. Her husband did not return.
Finally she had to surrender. Perhaps because she was
Fitz-Osbern's daughter and King William's kinswoman,
she was treated mercifully and given the customary forty
days grace before being outlawed. She sailed to Brittany
where she and her bridegroom were reunited. The powerful and wealthy Earl Ralf had lost everything in his bid for
yet more power. All his possessions in East Anglia, includ-
ing the borough of Norwich, reverted to the King. He was
fortunate, though, compared to poor Earl Waltheof whose
reward for 'information received' was to be beheaded
probably because he was an Englishman.

Inevitably there were other losers as a result of Lady
Emma's siege. These were the townsfolk, the innocent
bystanders who, as in any war, lost lives and property. And
afterwards when King William returned, Norwich 'was
assailed with indiscriminate revenge'. Was it, on a small
scale, another 'harrowing of the North'?

In Domesday Book – the survey made of William's
English kingdom to show him what revenues he could
obtain, and how conditions in 1086 compared to those of
1066 – we see some of the results of the Earl's ill-fated
rebellion. In 1066 Norwich was a prosperous borough with
1,320 burgesses rich enough to pay tax. Apart from King

Edward, it was the House of Godwin that exercised authority: Gyrth Godwineson, Earl of East Anglia; Harold
Godwineson, Earl of Wessex and former Earl of East
Anglia; Stigand, the Archbishop of Canterbury, who was
an old friend and faithful ally of the House of Godwin. To
these three the townsmen paid rents and duties.

By 1086 there were only 665 English burgesses who paid
tax. According to the Domesday Book entry, 'of the
burgesses who dwelt in the borough of Norwich, 22 have
gone away and dwell in Beccles . . . those fleeing, and the
others remaining have been entirely ruined'. There were
480 cottage-dwellers who did not pay tax 'on account of
poverty'. Properties stood empty all over the borough.

Ironically it was under Earl Ralf's guiding hand that the
market-place, which had been on Tombland, had been
moved to where we see it today. It was Earl Ralf who had
created the 'French Borough', a kind of 'new town',
thought to have been in the market area. There was 'a
certain church [there] which Ralf the Earl built', and which
was almost certainly the predecessor of St. Peter Mancroft.
Norwich and its people had been his pawns for a comparatively short space of time. Yet he had marked the place
indelibly. So had Emma in her own way. Breton Earl.
Norman lady. Neither of them lacked courage. Yet how the
English burgesses must have loathed them as they gazed
across the ruins of their houses to the castle, hated symbol of
the foreigners' domination.

Bishop Herbert

Bishop Herbert de Losinga came from a wealthy and well-connected family but we know neither the place nor the date of his birth. The latter has been placed somewhere between 1045 and 1050. His 'life', as far as we know it, started in a Benedictine abbey in Normandy, the abbey of Fécamp, to which he went as a young man, and of which he eventually became prior. He was holding that office in 1087 when William the Conqueror died.

The Conqueror's death complicated life for many people, for it meant the division once more of the England-Normandy kingdom. Robert Curthose, the Conqueror's eldest son, was allotted the Dukedom of Normandy. His younger brother, William Rufus, (the 'red-faced') became King of England. Those who held lands on both sides of the Channel did not know which of the two to support. Herbert de Losinga threw in his lot with William Rufus, who made him one of his chaplains and brought him to England to be Abbot of Ramsey. Herbert was then probably in his late thirties.

William Rufus may not have been as evil a man as he was painted by his enemies, the monkish chroniclers. Certainly after the death of his former guardian, Archbishop Lanfranc in 1089, his court became a very different one to that of his sober, pious father. High living at court and a military campaign to annexe Normandy meant that the King was always desperately in need of money. He looked on the Church as a handy source of revenue. When a see fell empty, he let it lie vacant for a few years while he drew the revenues. Then he sold it to the highest bidder. This was how the Bishopric of Thetford came to Herbert de Losinga in 1091. By the same 'deal' Herbert's father became Abbot of Winchester. It is said to have cost the pair £1,900. In his *Norwich Cathedral Past and Present (1910)* Herbert Leeds gives a translation of a long Latin verse supposedly written by a monkish contemporary of Bishop Herbert. It begins,

'In the Church arises a scandal;
Losinga is first the cause;
A sect is named for Simon,
And they scorn the Church's laws'.

There must have been many verses written about newly-appointed bishops at that time, for simony was the order of the day. Then in 1093 William Rufus made a very bad move. Mistakenly believing himself to be dying, he lost his nerve and appointed 'the saintly Anselm' as Archbishop of Canterbury. His mistake was to cost him dear. For Anselm was as strong and single-minded as he was upright. His appointment sent Herbert de Losinga hastening across the Channel, and to the King's fury, seeking an audience with the pope to be absolved for his sin of simony. With the papal blessing, and properly consecrated, Bishop Herbert came to Norwich in 1094, to where it had been decided to move the see.

According to the chronicles, even in late middle-age Bishop Herbert was a striking-looking man, 'handsome in his person and of bright countenance'. When he arrived in Norwich he was in good health and full of energy and vision. We can imagine him striding across those meadows beside the river, then called 'the Cowholm', a site which he had decided would be ideal for his new cathedral and the Benedictine monastery which would serve it. He obtained the meadows by charter from the King, and he negotiated with the rapacious Roger Bigod (Earl Ralf's successor) for that section of the Anglo-Saxon burgh which he needed for his precinct. This may have included a sizeable area of already vacant ground, one of the 'war-damaged' districts from the 1075 rebellion. It certainly did include St. Michael's Church and the Earl's Palace, both of which had to be demolished.

The First Register of Norwich Cathedral Priory tells us that, in addition to contributing funds of his own, Bishop Herbert then decreed, 'that a certain amount should be contributed from each message in this diocese for the construction of the work of Norwich church.' Thus began the Cathedral's first fund-raising campaign.

The original designer of Norwich Cathedral was not Bishop Herbert, but the anonymous master-mason whom he employed. This man would almost certainly have been a Norman and was probably known to the Bishop, at least by reputation. The master-mason was architect and clerk-of-works, responsible for collecting the labour force and for ordering the building materials. How the workmen were enlisted we do not know. They may have come willingly, anxious for employment, or they may have been 'pressed', particularly if they had skills which were in short supply. The unskilled labourers were probably English, the 'bosses' Norman. (We can see a parallel in the fact that local flint rubble was used for the core of the walls, but the fine white facing-stone was brought from Caen in Normandy). Who-ever they were, these workmen could not have come from Norwich itself. The population must have suddenly swelled. Accommodation had to be found for the free-masons and the roughmasons, for the wrights (or carpen-ters) who were to construct the timber roofs, for the 'plumbers', whose lead sheets would give the roof its waterproof covering, for the glaziers, and the decorators, and the men who manned the freight-barges and drove the carts.

Since land transport was expensive, as much of the building-material as possible was brought in by water. It was unloaded at a spot near the present Pull's Ferry and probably transported from there to the building-site along a narrow canal. There was so much of it too! Loads of flints for the rubble core of the walls. Boatloads of stone from the quarries of Caen. Sand and limestone for mortar. Great timbers for rafters and beams. Lead and iron.

Before the actual building could start the foundations had to be laid and the terrain examined to make sure it was solid enough. The master-mason, armed with lengths of rope, wooden pegs, and a measuring-stick would have marked out the ground-plan beforehand. One day in 1096 (the exact date has not been recorded) Bishop Herbert laid the foundation-stone, which was inscribed,

'In Nomine Patris et Filii Et Spiritus Sancti: Amen.
Ego Herbertus Episcopus Apposui Istum Lapidem'

('In the Name of the Father, the Son and the Holy Ghost, Amen.
I, Herbert the Bishop, have placed this Stone'.)

The stone was at the base of the Lady Chapel at the extreme eastern end of the church. This chapel may have been burned in the disastrous fire of 1170. It was certainly replaced by Bishop Walter de Suffield's Lady Chapel in the mid-thirteenth century and today the St. Saviour's Chapel partially covers the sites of both. So the Bishop's foundation-stone had a short life.

As the structure rose wooden scaffolding would have been put up. It was the roughmasons normally who laid the walls and the superior freemasons who chiselled and sculp-

Norwich Cathedral. The 15th century spire is the second tallest in England.

ted the facing-stone into shape. It was hazardous work for those who had to climb the scaffolding where a missed step might mean a fatal fall.

At this time the Benedictine monks whom Bishop Herbert had brought over from Normandy must have been living in a temporary wooden monastery. The Bishop had also founded a Benedictine priory on top of a hill on the other side of the Wensum. This was St. Leonard's Priory from which St. Leonard's Road takes its name. The English citizens of Norwich were now encircled by their hated foreign conquerors.

While Bishop Herbert's cathedral church was slowly taking shape, much was happening in the great world where he also had his rôle to play. In 1096 William Rufus finally came into possession of Normandy by paying Duke Robert ten thousand marks so that the latter could take part in Pope Urban's Crusade. In 1097 Archbishop Anselm was forced to leave the country, which allowed the King to draw the revenues of the vacant Archbishopric. But William Rufus did not have long to enjoy his ill-gotten gains. On 2nd August 1100 he was conveniently killed by a 'stray' arrow while hunting in the New Forest. His younger brother, Henry, who had been waiting in the wings, lost no time in claiming the throne. He was crowned on 5th August. As one of the chief primates of England, the Bishop of Norwich had to play his part in the coronation ceremonies and in the council-chambers. Yet he never lost his grip on the reins at home.

To Bishop Herbert the ideal Benedictine community was the one at Fécamp, of which he had been Prior. This was how he wanted the Norwich Cathedral Priory to be run. He wrote to the Abbé of Fécamp to ask for his co-operation; 'I have often purposed to send one or two brethren to Fécamp,' he explained, 'who might learn by personal inspection the practices . . . this, however, I thought, should only be done under your eye and by your permission . . . I send you one serving brother to tarry some little time in your kitchen; keep him with you and give orders that he be instructed in the secrets of that craft . . .'

De Losinga's *Letters* show that he took a lively interest in everything that went on in his monastery. The young scholars (the novices) were taught by him personally and he encouraged them to both read and write Latin verse. He would always give praise where it was due, but he was a strict disciplinarian: 'Youths, submit humbly to the correction of your schoolmaster,' he instructed the novices before one of his frequent absences, 'and when absent from me, prepare suitable answers to the examination which I shall hold when I am with you again.' The Bishop would not tolerate laziness in his pupils. 'I am sick of your delays,' he wrote sternly to Otto and Willelm, two novices, 'the fear in which you stood of me seems to have vanished; you were wont to supply me with four or five hundred lines once in every two or three days; now at the expiration of two or three months, there came twenty or thirty verses as inferior in polish as in number. . . .'

In a properly run Benedictine monastery the life of a monk was far from luxurious. Ideally his day was divided between prayer and work. At two o'clock in the morning the prior roused the sleeping men for the services of 'matins' and 'lauds'. They slept partly-clothed, their fur-lined 'night boots' by their side, so that they would not be late in arriving in church. At the end of the hour-long service, they went back to bed until the dawn service, 'Prime', which took place between six and seven a.m. Their breakfast of a little bread and wine was eaten in silence in the refectory.

At eight o'clock the 'Chapter Mass' was held, after which the monks went to the Chapter House to discuss the business of the day, and to discipline any of their number who confessed to misbehaviour. Punishment could vary

from being put on 'iron-rations' to being flogged or expelled. At eleven o'clock High Mass was celebrated. Then
the men went to the refectory to eat a vegetarian meal, again
in silence, while one of their brethren read to them from the
pulpit. The afternoon was given over to work. This could
mean any kind of labour, from copying out and illuminat-
ing manuscripts, to baking, brewing, or gardening. At six
o'clock in the evening they went to church for the service of
'Vespers'. After supper 'Compline' was recited, and they
went to bed in their communal dormitory about eight
o'clock.

It is not surprising that some of the brethren occasionally
fell by the wayside. Godfry was one to whom Herbert
wrote a stiff letter: 'You are, they say, seldom seen in the
cloister, often in the parlours; slow in resorting to the
church, swift in resorting to the grange and the public roads
which skirt it; you are constantly getting leave to have your
blood let, constantly getting leave to have a bath. . . . Is this
the recompense which you pledged yourself to make for the
love shown you, in receiving and sheltering in God's house
your aged father, and your son of seven years old?'

The Rule of Silence was obviously a difficult rule to
enforce: 'I do not lay upon you a burden which your
shoulders cannot bear,' the Bishop protested, 'You are free
to talk in your cloister, but only at the stated and customary
hours.'

Where the Rule of Chastity was concerned, discipline had
to be strict: 'I hear that there are some who are shocked . . .
who find fault with the severity of the penalties I inflict,'
Bishop Herbert wrote to Norman the Ostiary. 'In the house
of God, we cannot serve two masters. A lover of God
despises lust; a follower of lust knoweth not God.'

On occasions the Prior was brought sharply to heel: 'I am
informed that nothing is safe in your house,' de Losinga told
Prior Ingulf angrily, 'but that the Holy Church is polluted

by acts of theft proceeding from its own members. You lose books, cups, covers – everything except what is of no service to those who rob you . . . there have crept in unawares amongst you certain men to waste and consume the substance of your monastery.'

Outside the precinct there were also problems for de Losinga. He and his monastery were now part of the local political scene and he had to pay the penalty. He wrote bitterly to a friend about the multitude of treacherous officials – reeves, bailiffs, informers – against whom he had to wage a constant war. 'Their very friendship is a two-edged sword; and if at any time they remit something of their harsh claims, they make that indulgence a plea for devouring our substance with more than usual rapacity – their hands are full of blood, and they take notice of nothing but a bribe.'

In 1110 Bishop Herbert became Clerk of the Closet to Queen Edith Matilda, King Henry's first wife, who was always de Losinga's loyal friend. The Church was still at loggerheads with the Crown. Henry I had brought Anselm back from exile, only to find that the reinstated Archbishop of Canterbury was still to be a thorn in the royal flesh. Anselm now insisted that secular kings had no power to invest bishops and he refused to consecrate those bishops invested by Henry. For several years there was a stalemate between Primate and King, and Bishop Herbert must have been involved in many high-level discussions on this matter.

His heart must have soared when on 24th September 1101 his 'Church of Norwich' was finally consecrated. Incomplete as it was, the building could now be used for worship. Once choir and transept were complete, work started on the fortified Episcopal Palace on the Cathedral's north side, then on the monastic buildings on its south. By the time the Bishop died in 1119 his church was built as far as the twisted pillars. As befitted the Cathedral's founder, his body was laid before the high altar in a magnificent tomb. Both this tomb and its 18th century successor have gone. Today a black marble slab set in the floor before the altar marks Bishop Herbert's grave. Six iron candlesticks linked with white ropes stand guard around it. It is a fitting and beautiful monument for the man who wrote truthfully of his church and his monastery, 'remember, you enjoy this advantage at my expense, whose toils and labours have won it for you.'

1249

Recorded in the *Roll of the Crown Pleas* is the case of William Noche who came up before the King's Itinerant Judge at the Norwich Assizes of 1249. Noche's accuser, William Ribold, a criminal who was probably trying to save his own skin, said that, as well as knowing Noche to be a receiver of stolen goods, he had witnessed him killing a man called Joceline in his own house. Ribold claimed to have carried the body of Joceline out of the city and to have left it in Thorpe Wood. When Noche denied the accusation, Ribold asked that the case be settled 'by duel . . . body against body, according to the law of the land'. The law to which Ribold referred was the old feudal law which had used the ordeals of fire and water to prove or disprove a man's guilt. It was thirty-four years since the church had condemned this 'trial by lottery' but it was obviously still being used in the courts.

William Noche had no intention of hazarding his life in this primitive trial of strength and luck. He knew his rights as a citizen of Norwich. For the charter which Richard I had granted to the city in 1194 stated clearly that 'no persons shall be forced to duel or combat, but they may try all the pleas of the Crown among themselves, according to the custom of the City of London'. Noche claimed that any London citizen who was accused of a crime before the

King's Itinerant Judges, had the right to be 'tried' by thirty-six jurors of the city, eighteen from the north side of the river, and eighteen from the south. The accused had to swear, before the jurors, that neither he himself, nor his friends or relatives, had anything to do with the crime in question. If the thirty-six jurors brought in a unanimous verdict of 'Not Guilty', the accused was acquitted but if there were a single dissenting voice it meant a death-sentence. Noche, a citizen of Norwich, claimed the same right as a citizen of London.

Noche's claim was allowed. Eighteen jurors were summoned from Norwich-Over-The-Water, and eighteen from the southern side of the river. These men all found Noche 'Not Guilty' of the murder of Joceline.

Noche then demanded that on the second charge of felony he be tried by a common jury of twelve citizens. This too was allowed. The twelve again delivered a unanimous verdict of 'Not Guilty' and Noche was acquitted.

The year of Noche's trial saw another important event of quite a different sort in the city. This was the founding of the Great Hospital (then called St. Giles Hospital) by the Bishop of Norwich, Walter de Suffield. The Statutes of the Hospital which were confirmed in 1256 give us a lot of information about the institution and about those who ran it.

When the Hospital was founded it contained thirty beds, complete with sheets and bedding, and more were to be bought if the income of the Hospital increased. If any poor man who was ill or infirm came to the Hospital he was to be nursed there until he recovered. Any poor chaplain of the diocese of Norwich who had no means by which to support himself, or who was so old that he could no longer officiate, or who had a disease or incurable infirmity, was to be kept in the Hospital for as long as he lived. Thirteen poor people were to have their dinner there every day and to be allowed to warm themselves by the fire in winter-time. Seven poor scholars, named by the Master of the Grammar School (thought to have been situated somewhere near the 'Adam and Eve' pub) were also to have their daily dinner in the Hospital. There was to be a 'God's Box' in the building from which poor passers-by could be relieved. From Lady Day (25th March) to the Assumption (15th August) the great bell was to be rung each day at a determined hour for the distribution of bread, 'sufficient to repel hunger' to all the poor people then present. Whenever the Bishop of Norwich passed by the Hospital he gave his blessing to the sick there. That day the thirteen poor men were to have all their meals in the Hospital, and on the day following a Mass of the Holy Ghost was to be said for the welfare of the dead.

As regards the 'staff' of the Hospital it was to be governed by a Master. Four chaplains (all priests) were to conduct divine services in the choir with a deacon and a sub-deacon to assist them. Four Sisters, all at least fifty years of age, were to take care of the clothing, bedding, and other necessaries for the sick. The Master and chaplains were to live communally, eating in a refectory and sleeping in a dormitory. Four lay-brothers were also to be appointed to take care of the 'outside business' of the establishment.

These two accounts – of William Noche's trial and of Bishop Walter's foundation – show clearly the two contrasting faces of mid-13th century Norwich. Crime and violence on the one hand. Piety and charity on the other. All over the city there were small communities of good and holy men. The citizen walking along Conesford Street (today's King Street) would have passed Hildebrond's Hospital, named after its founder, Hildebrond the mercer. Here there were rooms for poor homeless people in a house supervised by a Master. (This Hospital had its own chapel in St. Edward's Church.) In the corner of St. Peter Parmentergate's churchyard he would have seen the House of the Pied

Friars, said to have been the only one of its kind in England. To the north of Rose Lane was the early establishment of the Grey Friars, who at the end of the century were to greatly enlarge their precinct and build a magnificent church.

Every district of Norwich had its religious community. At the southern end of Golden Ball Street in the churchyard of St. Martin's-in-the-Bailey (demolished in 1565) lived the small Fraternity of the Blessed Mary, St. Nicholas, and All the Saints. The Sack Friars had a House opposite St. Peter Hungate Church where Blackfriars Hall now stands. The Black Friars were still in their first House, north of the river, in Colegate. The White Friars settled in Cowgate in 1256, near St. James's Church in a house give to them by Philip de Cowgate, a merchant of the city. Where today's Assembly House stands was the College of the Chapel In The Fields, whose founder, John Le Brun, became its first Dean.

Yet this city, so well-endowed religiously, was far from tranquil. Francis Blomefield, the eighteenth-century historian, reading through the city records for 1263, found that 'so tumultuous was the city that I meet with many prosecutions of the citizens for firing one another's houses by night, cutting the bell-ropes off, that they should not ring when they had fired the houses, and suchlike . . . it was a dangerous time to live in.'[1]

Part of the reason for the frequent outbursts of violence in 13th Century Norwich lay in the general state of the nation. The reign of King John had been a disaster which culminated in the rebellion of the Barons. The Barons' ally, Prince Louis of France, had seized Norwich Castle in 1217 after King John's death and had plundered the city. In the 1260s there was another civil war with Simon de Montfort, King Henry III's brother-in-law, leading the rebellious barons. Norwich was to suffer at the hands of the latter

[1] *History of Norfolk*: Blomefield

St Helen's Church and Hospital, by James Sillett, 1828.
The Great Hospital was given to the city in 1547 as a
refuge for poor people. Today it is a home for the elderly.

when, defeated and 'disinherited', they raided the city in December 1266, kidnapped some of the wealthier citizens, and carried them off to a stronghold in the Isle of Ely.

The main cause behind much of the violence in the city had to do with its increasing prosperity and status. During this period the boroughs of medieval England were slowly progressing towards self-government. Wealth could buy privileges from the throne, enrolled in charters. What these 'privileges' did was to hand over the responsibilities of the city's government to the citizens and exclude the once-powerful royal officials, particularly the sheriff. By mid-century Norwich had the right to elect four Bailiffs and a Common Council to govern the city. The City Fathers were now responsible for gathering in the taxes and handing over a certain amount to the King (this had been the Sheriff's job). The city's legal affairs could be dealt with in the local court.

Materially Norwich was growing and thriving. It was a busy port, an important market-centre, and it had many trades and industries. It had a body of rich merchants who lived in fine stone houses. It had a Grammar School and its citizens were aware of the borough's status and of the privileges which were due to them as 'citizens of Norwich'. Yet in the midst of their borough were two sizeable areas which were virtually 'foreign' territories over which they had no rights. One belonged to the great stone castle whose Keeper represented the King. (When the City officials dared to enter the Castle 'Fee' in 1260 they had to beg for a royal pardon). The other belonged to the Cathedral Priory. It was with the latter that the citizens were most frequently involved in bitter, and sometimes violent, disputes throughout the century.

Although the citizens had no 'rights' in the Priory precinct the Prior had financial interests in the borough. The rectories of several of the city churches belonged to the

Priory. The common-land (later called Town Close) between Eaton and Harford Bridges, was the Priory's. The
monks claimed rights over Tombland and the fairs held
there. The city and the Priory both laid claim to Holmstrete
(now Bishopsgate Street) and its 'rates'. This led to a
situation in 1256 when the bailiffs collected the 'rates' for the
city one morning and the Prior's men collected the same
amount for the Priory in the afternoon.

No city coroner was allowed to hold an inquest on
anyone who had died in the Prior's Fee, no matter what the
circumstances. Thus (it was explained to the royal judge at
the Assize of 1251) there had been no inquest on Gerard
Goldfolde because he had drowned in a stretch of water
belonging to the Priory.

The frustration and anger of the citizens occasionally
found an outlet in violence. There was an attack on the
Priory in 1234 during which some buildings were burned
down and in the summer of 1272 the simmering hatred of
years finally erupted in murder and mayhem which was
recorded in the *Liber de Antiquis Legibus* of the Corporation
of London.

Norwich Riot

There are several different accounts of the Norwich riot of 1272 and of how it started. The monkish chronicler, Bartholomew Cotton, chose not to recount what led up to the citizens' attack on the priory. This makes one suspect that what most of the other chroniclers claim is true, that it was the monks who instigated the trouble. The conflict began in June 1272 at the Sunday Trinity Fair on Tombland. *The Roll of the Crown Pleas* gives the most detailed account of what happened here and since this was written down only fourteen years after the event, it may well be the real story.

A group of young men belonging to the borough came riding down to Tombland in the evening after dinner to the old churchyard of St. Michael's Church (the church which had been demolished in 1096 by Bishop Herbert). This piece of ground was just outside the priory gates. During the Fair stalls would have been set up here but most of the stallholders had now left and it seems that the area must normally have been a kind of 'recreation ground', for it housed a 'quintain' for the young men to tilt at. A quintain was constructed out of two pieces of wood. A vertical post hammered firmly into the ground supported a horizontal, swinging beam about six feet in length. At one end of the beam hung a heavy bag of sand, at the other, a small, square board. The young horsemen would 'charge' the quintain, lances at the ready, and try to strike the board and pass through before the sandbag hit them from behind. It sounds like good harmless fun for a summer evening but on this particular evening the fun was short-lived. A quarrel started between the priory servants who were at the scene and some of the citizens. In the fight that followed at least one Norwich citizen, probably more, was killed by the men of the priory.

The Norwich coroner held an inquest and found the priory servants guilty of murder. According to some versions he held the inquest in the prior's fee, to others he had the two priory servants arrested the first time they crossed the boundary between priory and borough. Whichever is true, the effect on the prior was the same. He was furious and he had the whole city excommunicated for breach of his privileges. He then shut up the priory gates and stationed his men along the wall. We are told in *The Roll of the Crown Pleas* that the monks hung 'scutcheons, targets and bucklers' over the gates and shot with their crossbows at passing citizens.

This state of affairs lasted until August when there was a sudden dramatic escalation in the hostilities. A gang of priory servants left the precinct one Sunday evening and went on the rampage. They robbed a city merchant, Alfred Cutler, of more than £20 which was a vast amount of money in those days. They broke into a tavern owned by a citizen called Hugh de Bromholm and, having drunk all they could, they deliberately let the rest of the wine drain out of the casks.

As far as the city was concerned, this was the last straw. The four Bailiffs and the Common Council had 'an emergency meeting'. They sent a letter to the King complaining bitterly about the activities of the prior's men. They called all the citizens to a meeting the following morning in the market-place. Their intention was to set up some sort of militia with a view to warding off further attacks by the monks. Unfortunately their fellow citizens were in no mood to appreciate the wisdom of such an idea.

In view of what happened subsequently it is interesting to learn a little about the kind of men who were 'running' the city in 1272. John le Brun, for example. He was the town clerk. He was also the Dean of the College of the Chapel in the Fields which he had founded. He and his two brothers, Matthew and Jeffrey, had each inherited four acres of land in Chapel Field and the living of a city church, so they were obviously a fairly well-off family.

John le Scot was one of the Common Council and sufficiently rich to be able to give two houses 'in the Cock Row' to the Hospital of St. Giles.

John Knot, another of the Council, presented the Hospital of St. Paul with 6s 8d rent 'out of divers houses in Norwich'.

William de Dunwich, one of the Bailiffs was an important and wealthy man whose name crops up in many legal transactions around this time. In 1259 he had bought the handsome house which had been built by Jurnet the Jew in Conesford Street, (part of which is incorporated in today's Wensum Lodge). In the same year he also bought 'The Stone House' in Conesford Street. In 1261 he gave the Black Friars one of his gardens which abutted on to their precinct in Colegate. In 1271 he was a witness to the Foundation Charter of the Sack Friars. After the death of his wife he gave by deed to the Great Hospital his meadow by Bishop's Bridge which extended from the river to the Hospital, 6s 8d rent in Holme Street, three properties in Conesford, 'and many rents of value, payable out of the houses in most of the parishes in the city'. In his will in addition to other bequests, he gave a large sum of money to maintain five sick people in the Hospital continually.

These then were the rich, devout gentlemen who had

The Ethelbert Gateway. Built by the citizens in atonement for the 1272 Riot, it was completed in 1316.

summoned the citizens together on that August morning of 1272. One can hardly imagine that they would incite the crowd to violence. Someone did, however. Soon the mob was sweeping down from the market-place to Tombland howling for revenge. It is at this point that the monk, Bartholomew Cotton, begins his account of the riot. Naturally he dwells on the iniquities of the citizens: 'They fired the great gates with reed and dry wood and burnt them down, with St. Albert's Church (i.e. St. Ethelbert's Church) which stood near them, and all the books in it . . . they fired the great almonry and church doors and great tower. . . . Others got upon St. George's steeple and threw fire with slings, and fired the great belfry beyond the quire so that the whole church was burnt, all but the Virgin Mary's Chapel'.

It was proved that the tower of the Cathedral had been accidentally set on fire by monks who were preparing weaponry to use against the citizens. Cotton may not be very reliable either on his assessment of the number of casualties sustained by the priory: 'sub-deacons, clerks, and some laymen were killed in the cloister and precinct . . . others were carried out and killed in the city'. What he and the other chroniclers agree on is that the prior soon left the scene of battle and headed for Yarmouth.

Not that Prior William de Burnham (or Brunham) was running away. For whatever he lacked it was not courage. He went to Yarmouth to gather a 'posse' of armed men with whom he returned to Norwich (by barge, some say). He arrived in the city 'with trumpet blown and sword in hand' and proceeded to harry the place, 'wounding, killing, and destroying many (citizens) and their houses'.

King Henry III and Bishop Roger de Skerning became extremely alarmed. The king called a meeting of his bishops and nobles for 1st September at Bury St. Edmunds, 'to advise him how to proceed against the citizens for these heinous transgressions'. The bishop convened his clergy at Eye in Suffolk on 30th August and by general consent an excommunication was published against the city of Norwich, the four Bailiffs, all the members of the Common Council, and certain others being specifically named.

There was cause for fear when King Henry arrived in the city on 14th September for his was a punitive visit. The sentences he passed on those rioters who had been arrested were barbaric and horrible. Over thirty of them were dragged about the streets by horses until they were dead. Others were hung, drawn, and quartered, and their bodies later burned. The woman who had allegedly set fire to the priory gate was burned alive, (the old Anglo-Saxon punishment for arson). Twelve citizens forfeited all their possessions to the King. The prior was committed to the Bishop's prison for having murdered a citizen and his lands were confiscated.

This was not the end of the city's punishment. Norwich had to pay, literally, for its misdeeds. Meanwhile it lost all its privileges. The four Bailiffs were dismissed and 'Keepers', (appointed by the king) put in their place. Until it made restitution to the Cathedral Priory the whole city remained under an interdict, excluded from the sacraments of the church. Two months later the King who had passed this heavy sentence lay dead. In December one of the chief protagonists, William de Dunwich, died too. The citizens of Norwich still had not paid any money to the priory. It looked as though they had no intention of ever doing so.

It was not until 1274 that the affair was resolved. Edward I laid down the terms for a settlement, and to these the city finally agreed. For six years they paid 500 marks a year towards the rebuilding of Norwich Cathedral church. They gave to the same church a pyx (or cup) weighing ten pound in gold, and worth £100 in money, to serve at the sacrament at the High Altar. They promised to make new gates into the priory, and to send some of their chief citizens to Rome to assure the pope of their good faith. King Edward restored the city's privileges. In December 1275 the bishop took off the interdict. Finally, in 1276 the pope's General Absolution was published on Palm Sunday by the Priors of the Grey Friars and the Black Friars. Norwich's spiritual night was over.

Margaret Paston

The ruined tower known as Drayton Lodge stands just off Drayton High Road on the outskirts of Drayton village. It played an important part in the life of one notable lady of the fifteenth century, the redoubtable Margaret Paston.

Margaret's husband was John Paston. He was nineteen years old (and Margaret was about the same age) when they married in 1440. Judge William Paston, John's father, had been a clever and ambitious man of North Norfolk yeoman stock. He had elevated the Paston family to the rank of county gentry and had bought up lordships and property in different parts of Norfolk. To his son and heir, John, fell the task of holding on to the family estates in a lawless and rapacious age. It was a task which had necessarily to be shared by Margaret during her husband's frequent absences in London and elsewhere.

Miraculously many hundreds of letters have survived out of the correspondence of this remarkable family, dating from c. 1420 to 1503. Scholars treasure them because they give such a comprehensive picture of life in a medieval 'gentry' household. The *Paston Letters* (published in several different editions) are not for scholars only. They are for anyone who is interested in human nature. The personality of Margaret, in particular, is clearly projected through the medium of her correspondence. Her cares and her joys are

comprehensible, never remote. They are the same experi-
enced by wives and mothers today. Thus in September 1443
young Margaret, (mother of a year-old boy, and probably
expecting her second child) was distressed by the news that
her twenty-two year old husband had been ill: 'I had never
so heavy a season as I had fro the time that I wost of your
sickness till I wost of your amendment . . . if I might have
had my will, I should have seen you ere this time. I would ye
wern at home – if it were your ease, and your sore might
been as well looked to here as it is there – liefer than a new
gown, though it were of scarlet.'

After twenty-five years of marriage Margaret was still
'mine own dear sovereign lady' to her husband. When she
had parted from him after a sojourn in the Fleet Prison
(where John was temporarily confined through the
machinations of his enemies) he wrote to her, playfully, and
tenderly, in verse:

> 'My Lord Percy and all this house
> recommend them to you, dog, cat, and mouse,
> and wish ye had be here still,
> for they say ye are a good gill.'

Margaret had seven surviving children with whom she
was sometimes pleased, sometimes exasperated, about
whom she complained or worried, just as mothers have
always done. Her daughter Marjorie caused her most heart-
ache, by marrying the family-steward, Richard Calle, after
becoming secretly betrothed to him. It was a love-match
and a good marriage but not what Marjorie's family had
planned for her. Margaret and John's eldest son, John II,
rarely managed to please his father and often vexed Margaret as well. John II was always running out of 'funds',
particularly after he had been found a place in the household
of King Edward IV:

'I suppose ye understand that the money that I had of you
at London may not endure with me till that the King go into

Wales and come again . . .', he wrote anxiously to his father in August 1461.

The practical management of the Paston properties, and of the household in general devolved largely on Margaret. She had to order provisions and fuel and animal-fodder, supervise the buying and selling of houses, and see to it that the whole family were well, and fashionably clothed. 'As touching your liveries' she wrote to John from Norwich in 1455, 'there can none be got here of that colour that ye would have of, neither murry, nor blue, nor good russets, underneath 4s the yard at the lowest price, and yet is there not enough of one cloth and colour to serve you'.

Margaret and John's parish church was St. Peter's Hungate (now a museum) and their principal town house seems to have been that on Elm Hill which was to be destroyed in the fire of 1507. (Today we can admire the 16th century house which Augustine Steward built on the site.) In 1451 Margaret was obviously looking for another property in Norwich. She was related to Robert Toppes, a wealthy merchant and four times Mayor of the city, who had had the impressive Dragon Hall built in Conesford Street [today's King Street] c. 1450. On 3rd June 1451 Margaret reported to John: 'It was told me this week that there is a fair place to sell in St. Lawrence parish . . . near the church, and by the water side, the which place Toppes hath to sell. Pyte, a lyster, [i.e. a dyer] bought it of Toppes and now, for default of payment, Toppes hath entered again therin, and shall sell it in haste, as it is told me. The said lyster dwelleth therein at this time, but he shall [be put] out . . . I suppose if ye like to buy it when ye come home, ye might have it of Toppes cheap, or better than another should'.

It was during the major crises in her husband's life that Margaret showed her real mettle. As early as 1449 she had been left to defend the manor-house of Gresham, four miles from Cromer – a property which her late father-in-law had bought from Thomas Chaucer. Lord Moleyns, urged on by the Pastons' enemies, laid claim to Gresham and in January 1449 he launched an attack on the house. Outnumbered, Margaret and her servants could not withstand the invasion. According to John Paston's petition to the King

Drayton Lodge. This last remnant of a Paston manor stands on a hill above the Wensum.

demanding redress, Moleyns' men had 'mined down the wall' of Margaret's chamber and had then carried her bodily out of the house.

Margaret had experience behind her when in 1465 she found herself in the position of 'captainess' (her own term)

of the Paston forces during a summer of hostilities instigated by John de la Pole, Second Duke of Suffolk. Her
husband was in London embroiled in the litigation that had
followed the death of his patron, Sir John Fastolf. By
Fastolf's bequest Paston had inherited, among other properties, the manors of Drayton and Hellesdon, whose inhabitants now owed him both rents and allegiance. Those who
were challenging Fastolf's bequests found a willing tool
in the powerful Duke of Suffolk. Lord of the manor of
Costessey, he was looking with greedy eyes on the neighbouring manors of Hellesdon and Drayton. Doubtless
he thought it would be an easy matter to annex them,
especially when he had only a woman to reckon with.

In April 1465 Margaret was living at Caister Castle,
another inherited property which the Pastons had continually to defend. From here she sent John a legal deed
which they both believed would refute Suffolk's claim to
the manor of Drayton. By May when the situation was no
less ominous Margaret decided to take up residence in the
Hellesdon manor-house where she and John had lived
periodically since Fastolf's death in 1459. She rode to
Drayton to talk to the tenantry in an attempt to keep their
allegiance. Most she reckoned were loyal, but there were
one or two 'false shrews'. Suffolk's local agent was Philip
Lipyate, Rector of Salle, and he was already stirring up
trouble. He had seized the horse of a man called Dorlet, who
worked for the Pastons, as he ploughed his land in Drayton,
saying that it was in lieu of a year's rent. 'But I trowe to get
Dorlet his horse again, or else Mr. Philip is like to be
unhorsed', Margaret promised John in her letter.

Margaret's next report was sent to John on 10th May. She
had sent four servants to Drayton to collect the rents from
the villagers. No doubt in retaliation for the seizure of
Dorlet's horse, the Paston servants had taken two plough-
horses belonging to Piers Warren, who was a crony of

Philip Lipyate's and of the bailiff of Costessey. They had brought these horses back to Hellesdon.

Had Margaret any idea what would happen next? She does not say. She gives only an objective account of how, the following morning, Lipyate and the bailiff of Costessey came riding into Hellesdon at the head of more than eight-score men. The numbers were obviously intended to intimidate. They certainly were not needed to seize four plough-horses – two belonging to the parson (value four marks), and two to a man called Thomas Stermyn (value forty shillings). Margaret decided to enlist the help of William Skipwith, who was Member of Parliament for Norwich. Together they paid a visit to the Bishop of Norwich, Walter Lyhart, to lay a complaint against Lipyate, who as Rector of Salle came under the Bishop's jurisdiction. The Bishop expressed sympathy and support for the Pastons while admitting to a dislike and a distrust of Lipyate. To judge from subsequent events he does not seem to have had much control over Lipyate's actions. When Margaret wrote to her husband on 10th May Lipyate appears to have been installed in the manor-house at Drayton for she reported anxiously that 'On Thursday all day there were kept in Drayton lodge (as many as) 60 persons, and yet . . . there be within daily and nightly . . . 16 or 20 persons'. She guessed rightly that these retainers of the Duke were awaiting an opportunity to attack Hellesdon. And she had also heard 'that Thomas Ellis (Mayor of Norwich) said at Drayton that if my Lord of Suffolk need a hundred men he would purvey him thereof, and if any man of the town would go to Paston he would do lay them fast in prison'.

Naturally the Drayton tenants, having had one master intruded upon them, were neither willing nor able to pay rents to another. Margaret wrote to John on 20th May to tell how, on the previous Saturday, she had sent four of her men to Drayton to seize seventy-seven head of cattle in lieu of unpaid rents. The cattle had been driven to Hellesdon and shut in the pinfold. When their unfortunate owners arrived at the Hellesdon manor-house demanding the return of their beasts they were told they would have them again only when they had paid their rents.

At this point a new character stepped on to the scene. On the day when Margaret seized the Drayton cattle, William Harleston, Esq. of Denham in Suffolk, (Under-Steward of the Duchy of Lancaster, and trusted retainer of the Duke of Suffolk) happened to be in Norwich. As soon as he heard what had happened he summoned the poor harassed Drayton tenantry to threaten them with dire retribution should they pay any rents to the Pastons. He then arrived 'at even-song time' at Hellesdon, and proposed to Margaret Paston that each side should return the several distraints they had taken and eschew any more conflict. Margaret was not to be persuaded. To maintain her husband's claim on Drayton manor she had to keep pressing for her rents. The following afternoon a writ was served by the Sheriff of Norfolk which Margaret could not ignore. The seventy-seven cattle were back in Drayton by the evening.

By the end of June it was clear that Lipyate was preparing to invade Hellesdon. John Paston saw how important it was for his wife to constantly fan the flames of allegiance in his imperilled estates: 'ye be a gentlewoman and it is worship (i.e. right) for you to comfort your tenants; wherefore I would ye might ride to Hellesdon and Drayton and Sparham, and tarry at Drayton and speak with them, and bid them hold with their old master till I come,' he told Margaret on 27th June. But Margaret was having to undertake tasks more arduous than talking to the tenantry, as Richard Calle, Paston's steward informed his master on 10th July. The previous Monday Lipyate and the bailiff of Costessey had marched into Hellesdon with three hundred men. Luckily Margaret had been forewarned and with John

II to help her she had successfully defended the manor-house with forty men and guns. Paston's retainers were being continually harassed, threatened, and physically assaulted by Suffolk's men to Margaret's anxiety and distress. She wrote to John asking him to try to find some solution for the unhappy situation they were in. That she was ill at this stage we learn from John's anxious letter of 13th July in which he refers to her being 'sickly' and begs her to 'take what may do your ease and spare not.'

But 'sickly' or not Margaret had to 'captain' her forces again on 1st August, (Lammas Day) when the Drayton Manor Court was to sit. It was vital that a Paston official should be in the chair of authority if their claim to the manor was to be upheld. She had a job to find two men brave enough to challenge the authority of the powerful Duke. In the end the Paston's family chaplain, Sir James Gloys, agreed to go with another faithful retainer, Thomas Bond. On 7th August Margaret wrote to tell John what had happened. In the manor yard where the court was kept, Bond and Gloys had confronted the Suffolk faction – Lipyate and co. with sixty retainers, plus the 'fickle' Drayton tenantry armed with rusty pole-axes and billhooks – and had announced they had come to hold the court in Paston's name. How courageous! But how foolhardy. In a short time poor Bond was on his way to Costessey under arrest, 'his arms (bound) behind him with whip-cord like a thief'. Margaret acted quickly. Early next morning she rode into Norwich to confront the royal judges before they went to the Shire House to hold the Assizes. In front of all the great ones of the county she made her complaint against the agents of the Duke of Suffolk. And to her immense satisfaction she witnessed the hated Bailiff of Costessey publicly receiving 'a great rebuke' from a sympathetic judge. The Sheriff of Norfolk was ordered to investigate what was happening in Drayton and

Hellesdon, and that evening Thomas Bond was set free.

It was following this that Margaret went, at John's request, to join him in his quarters in the Fleet Prison. Her second son, 'Little John', or John III, who was then twenty-one years old, was left in charge of 'the garrison' at Hellesdon. There appear to have been no disturbances during Margaret's absence.

The Duke of Suffolk was biding his time. He struck in mid-October having arrived in Norwich with five hundred men. Hellesdon manor house was ransacked. Margaret told her husband the sorrowful tale in a letter dated 27th October: 'they made your tenants of Hellesdon and Drayton, with others, to help to break down the walls of the place and the lodge both, God knoweth full evil against their wills . . . the Duke's men ransacked the church and bare away all the goods that was left there, both of ours and of the tenants . . . they stood upon the high altar and ransacked the images . . . and put away the parson out of the church till they had done, and ransacked every man's house in the town five or six times . . . And as for lead, brass, pewter, iron, doors, gates, and other stuff of the house, men of Cossey and Cawston have it, and that they might not carry, they have hewn it asunder'.

Even in that lawless age the sacking of Hellesdon caused a sensation: 'There cometh much people daily to wonder thereupon, both of Norwich and of other places, and they speak shamefully thereof. The Duke had be better than £1000 that it had never be done,' Margaret told John. Loyal wife as she was, did she reflect, as she looked upon the ruins of Hellesdon, on what the Bishop had said to her six months before: 'that he would not abide the sorrow and trouble that ye [i.e. John] have abiden to win all Sir John Fastolf's goods.'

John Paston died in May 1466, in London, aged forty-five. Margaret survived him by eighteen years.

Queen Elizabeth I

The Mayor and aldermen of Norwich were informed in 1578 that 'her Majesty designed a progress through Norfolk and Suffolk, and to visit this city'. According to a pamphlet entitled *The Receyving of the Queenes Majestie into hir Highnesse Citie of Norwich*, a compilation of contemporary accounts of the visit, the feverish preparations for the royal visit began in June. At the Mayor's Court, on the twentieth of that month, it was ordered that the streets, lanes, and houses should be repaired and beautified, and letters were sent to Yarmouth and Lynn asking for a loan of labourers.

The work seems to have started shortly afterwards. The Queen was to enter the city by St. Stephen's Gate, so the road to it was 'new gravelled'. The gate itself was completely refurbished, fitted with a new portcullis and painted with symbolic emblems. On the outer side the Queen's arms were resplendent above a falcon, her favourite badge, and both were flanked by a Cross of St. George and the arms of the city. On the inner face of the gate was painted the red rose of York, and the white rose of Lancaster with a red-and-white rose between them. Underneath, in verse, was the customary piece of flattery designed to bring a smile to the royal lips:

> 'Division kindly stryfe
> Blest union quench'd the Flame
> Thence sprang our noble PHAENIX deare,
> The pearlesse Prince of FAME'

Sufficiently close to St. Stephen's Gate to be within sniffing distance of the 'pearlesse Prince' was one of the city's grand muck-hills. This stood at what was then called Brazen Doors (now the corner of Grove Road and Queens Road) near the Swine Market on All Saints Green. Such an embarrassment could not be allowed while the Queen was in the city. It was carted away.

In the heart of the city the Market Place had to be smartened up. The Market Cross (no mere 'cross', of course, but a handsome little building around ten metres wide and twenty metres high) was painted white, with its posts 'timber-coloured'. The stocks and pillory which stood beside the Guildhall were removed. At the Maddermarket, through which the Queen would pass on her way to the Cathedral, the wall of St. John's Churchyard was taken down and rebuilt, to make the thoroughfare wider.

The Queen was to be in residence at the Bishop's Palace for six days, during which an appearance of salubriousness had to be maintained. To this end, occupations that gave rise to unpleasant smells were to be suspended. No cows were to be brought into the city. Grocers must not melt down tallow. The wool-scourers were forbidden to wash dirty fleeces.

A programme of entertainments had to be arranged and in July a 'master of revels' was sent for. He was Master Thomas Churchyard, who was by no means the insignificant nincompoop that some commentators would make out. In 1578 Churchyard was in his late fifties. In his youth he had been page to Henry Howard, the poet-Earl of Surrey, who in 1540 had had a mansion built in the city, (in today's Surrey Street). Churchyard was probably well-acquainted with Norwich. He had served as a soldier for several years in France, Ireland, Scotland, and the Low Countries, before becoming attached in minor capacities to the Court and its circle. He was certainly well-known. In

1557 he had had poems included in the prestigious *Tottel's Miscellany* along with such poets as Wyatt, Surrey and Chaucer. In 1563 he had contributed a tragedy, *Shore's Wife*, to the highly-acclaimed *Mirror For Magistrates*. And in 1579 he was to publish another 'best-seller', the *Generall Rehearsall of Warres*, based on his own experiences as a soldier. His personal account of the Queen's visit to Norwich is very comical in parts and some read this as unintentional humour.

Churchyard was sent for to assist the Norwich City Fathers. 'I was the fyrste that was called,' he tells us, 'and came to Norwiche aboute that businesse, and remayned there three long weekes before the Courte came thether, devising and studying the best I coulde for the Citie; albeit other gentlemen, as Maister Goldingham, Maister Garter, and others, dyd steppe in after.'

What Churchyard devised was a programme of daily entertainments to be interspersed among the civic orations and presentations. These took the conventional form of pageants and masques, a couple of the latter to be performed on the nearby river. Master Garter, a minor poet, wrote the verse for most of the pageants. Master Goldingham was responsible for the spectacular masque performed at the Bishop's Palace on the eve of the Queen's departure. Music was to be provided by the renowned 'City Waits'.

The Mayor's Court arranged all the civic ceremonies. On 2nd August it was agreed that forty 'bachelors' should be appointed to wait upon the mayor, aldermen, and justices when they met the Queen. In the event sixty handsome young men of the city were mustered. They wore black satin doublets, black hose, black taffeta hats with yellow bands, and coats of purple taffeta trimmed with lace and led the procession out of the city in the early afternoon of Saturday 16th August. Their destination was Harford Bridges where the Queen was to be met and formally

The Bishop's Palace Gate. The 15th century gateway is
little changed from when Elizabeth passed through it to
her lodgings at the Palace. The wider entrance is for
carriages, the other for pedestrians.

welcomed to Norwich. Behind the purple coats of the bachelors came the scarlet gowns of the Mayor and aldermen, the scarlet cloaks of the former mayors, and the violet gowns of the former sheriffs. The principal citizens followed, wearing their best velvet coats and mounted on their finest horses. Then came a 'strong-arm' rearguard to act as a buffer between the privileged and the 'hoi polloi' and to prevent the latter from 'disturbing the arraye'.

They all waited at Harford Bridges for over an hour before the Queen finally came into view with her 'very great trayne, eight of the privy councill, divers noble personages . . . and three French Imbassators', (as the Mayor's Court Book tells us). The Mayor, Robert Wood, a wealthy grocer, had his Latin oration and the civic gift at the ready. Neither would have been any surprise to Elizabeth. It was the custom to greet her with a speech in Latin. It was also customary to present her with a silver-gilt cup full of money. The surprise may have lain in the amount of money there was in the cup. Some towns could afford only a meagre twenty pounds. But Norwich, the second city in the realm, managed to raise a hundred. After the cheering had died down the Mayor made his speech and handed over the cup.

The Sword of the City was then relinquished to Elizabeth and on her behalf a silver mace was presented to the Mayor. He carried it before the Queen as the procession set off towards the city. Before they reached the walls they encountered the first of Churchyard's 'diversions'. A young man dressed as 'King Gurgunt', the mythical founder of Norwich and builder of the castle, was stationed with his attendants at a spot on the city common or 'Town Close' from which the castle was clearly visible. Very splendid they were too in their green-and-white silks and black velvet. It was probably Churchyard who had written Gurgunt's speech. He had taken care of everything – except the weather. As Gurgunt spoke the first of his forty-two lines – 'Leave of to muse, most gracious Prince of English soile' – a torrential shower sent his audience galloping off towards the shelter of the city.

Sadly for the 'Master of the Revels' this was only the first of several abortive entertainments. The whole of Monday's programme had to be cancelled because of rain. The elaborate water-masque planned for Wednesday evening had to be cancelled. And when Churchyard tried, on the Thursday, to stage a double water-event, to make up for the cancellation, a thunderstorm of such violence exploded over the poor actors' heads that they were literally washed off the stage. 'We were so dashed and washed that it was a greater pastime to see us look like drowned rats than to have the uttermost of the shows rehearsed,' Churchyard recounted ruefully.

But the Queen's visit was not all rain and despondency. There were several highlights. The Master of the Grammar School, Stephen Lymbert, made a great hit with Elizabeth. The young man was standing at the door of the Great Hospital in Bishopsgate on the Wednesday evening waiting for the Queen to pass on her way back from Mount Surrey. She obviously took to him at first sight, for as she approached, she called reassuringly, 'Be not afraid.' Stephen, with great aplomb, replied, 'I thanke your Majestie for your good encouragement.' Then he got down on one knee to begin his Latin oration. As he did so, Elizabeth sharply called the three French ambassadors and some of her English lords to order, exhorting them to 'harken!' She listened attentively herself to a speech in which Lymbert thanked her for a gift to the Great Hospital of certain lands at Cringleford. When he had finished, she declared, 'It is the best that ever I heard; you shall have my hande.' Thereupon she pulled off her glove and the schoolmaster got to his feet, bent low, and kissed the royal fingers. Later the Queen sent

St Benedict's Gate from a drawing by John Ninham, 1792. Also known as Westwyk Gate and occasionally adorned with the heads or 'quarters' of traitors. An orator made a farewell speech to Elizabeth from a stage covered with a cloth of gold and crimson velvet.

back to ask for Lymbert's name, a mark of high favour.

Goldingham's masque which was performed on the Thursday evening was also a success, mainly because each character in it presented the Queen with an attractive gift. 'Jupiter' presented the first one – 'a riding wand of whale's fin, curiously wrought'. There were seven more gifts, each increasing in value, before the pièce de résistance, which was 'Cupid's' offering of a solid gold arrow.

The most important of all the entertainments laid on for the Queen was perhaps the first pageant she saw, just after she entered the city on Saturday afternoon. Pageants had been used for a long time as vehicles through which the people could communicate their sentiments to the sovereign. In this case, the pageant in St. Stephen's Street was presented by the 'Artizan-Strangers', but it made a statement from the entire city to the Queen.

The 'Strangers' were the Dutch and Walloon cloth-workers who in the preceding twenty-four years had come in to the city in ever increasing numbers. They had come for two reasons. Many of them, as Protestants, had been fleeing Spanish religious persecution. On the other hand, some far-sighted men in Norwich had seen that weavers from across the North Sea might save the city's dying textile industry. The Strangers had skills the Norwich weavers did not possess. Their woollen cloths known as 'russells' and 'sateens' had, for many years, been ousting Norwich worsteds from markets abroad. So Norwich had virtually 'invited' the Strangers to settle in the city. By 1578 there were about 6000 of them.

The Strangers' settlement had not been without its problems. There was an amount of understandable jealousy and suspicion on the part of the local weavers. In the summer of 1570 certain local Roman Catholic gentry had used the Strangers' presence in the city as a pretext for trying to incite rebellion. On two occasions the nucleus of a rebel army assembled in Norwich. Fortunately there was no local support. The rebel leaders were arrested and comparatively little harm was done.

The Government had been alarmed. After all Norwich was the second city in the realm. No doubt there were some misgivings in the city too. Had it been a wise step to take in so many Strangers, and perhaps cause serious unrest among the local populace? The Artizan-Strangers' Pageant was the reply to that question and the city's vindication of its action to the Queen.

The forty-foot long platform had been positioned at the foot of a bank against which an artificial 'freestone wall' had been erected. The 'writing on the wall' assured Her Majesty that her city of Norwich was now all that she desired. It read as follows:

> The causes of this Commonwealth are,
> > God truely preached,
> Justice duely executed,   The people obedient
> Idleness expelled   Labour cherished
> > Universall Concorde preserved.

On the panel between the platform and the ground were painted pictures of seven looms with seven weavers turning out different cloths. On the stage itself eight small girls stood at one end spinning worsted yarn and eight sat at the other end knitting worsted yarn hose. The rest of the stage was occupied by weavers displaying the kind of cloths that they made. A child representing 'Commonwealth' 'a pretie boy richly apparelled' had to speak the all-important verses to the Queen. These had been written by Master Garter and although not great poetry they undoubtedly made their point:

'So weak we were within this dozen yeare' could apply equally to the Strangers and to Norwich itself.

The last verse is an unambiguous assertion of Norwich's present prosperity:

> 'We bought before the things that now we sell,
> These slender ympes their workes do passe the waves,
> God's peace and thine, we holde and prosper well,
> Of every mouth the handes the charges saves.
> Thus through thy helpe and ayde of power devine,
> Doth Norwich live, whose harts and goods are thine.'

The Queen seems to have been both highly gratified and intensely interested in this pageant. She looked with particular attention at the children's knitting and spinning, closely examined the looms and admired their different products, then gave the actors 'greate thankes', before she went on her way.

The following Tuesday the Strangers were able to return that thanks. The minister of the Dutch church in the city presented the Queen with an engraved cup worth £50 and delivered yet another long Latin oration. The nub of this speech was the Strangers' gratitude that the Queen had allowed them to settle 'in this thy citie of Norwich, which thy Majestie hath of clementie graunted unto us for a mansion-place, which were banished for Christ his religion,' and also 'that we finde the minds of the people favourable towards us.'

Entertaining Elizabeth was not just a question of keeping her amused. This most astute of politicians was enjoying a 'working' holiday, 'doing the rounds' to make sure her domain was in order. It was up to her hosts to demonstrate that this was so. Norwich passed that test with flying colours.

Anguish's School

Anguish's School was an important institution in Norwich from the seventeenth century onwards. The property in which the original school was housed was in Fishergate. Most of it was demolished in the 1930s, and the Master's house with its handsome porch in the 1960s. Thomas Anguish was Mayor of Norwich in 1611. In his will, dated 1617, he bequeathed a house and other property 'for a hospital or conveniente place for the keepinge, bringinge up, and teachinge of younge and very poore children . . . (who) have not friends to help them'. 'A hospital' in 17th Century terminology meant a charitable institution. From the entry of 13 November 1620 in the Assembly Book we can see how Anguish's bequest was carried out. The rooms on the east side of his house were to be immediately fitted out to receive the orphans and ten boys and two girls were to be admitted at the discretion of the Mayor and the Court of Aldermen. The children were to be supplied with two suits of clothes, one of linen and one of wool, by their parish or ward and they were to be educated both in work and learning at the discretion of the Hospital's supervisor. Eight beds were to be provided, six for the twelve above-mentioned children, and two to be kept in reserve. The entry of 25th October 1620 in the Mayor's Court Book lists the children's diet. Each child was to receive every day fourteen ounces of bread. On Mondays, Wednesdays, Fridays and Saturdays they were each to be given five ounces of cheese and two-and-a-half ounces of butter, but on Sundays, Tuesdays and Thursdays they were to have pease and pottage instead. Each child was to be allowed half a barrel of beer a week in the winter and three firkins of beer weekly in the summer.

According to the Court Book on 30th December 1620 Christopher Giles was appointed keeper at the Hospital. He was allowed £4 a head to feed the children and 5 marks a year for coal. The newly appointed schoolteacher, Nicholas Shaxton, whose specific job was to teach reading and writing, would be given either a salary of 53/4d a year or a rent-free house to the same value.

Despite the earlier resolution to admit ten boys and two girls, on 17 January 1621 the Hospital seems to have contained boys only. These were: Thomas Hampling and John Mott, both aged 7; Robert Mard and Alexander Grey, both aged 8 'or thereabouts'; Martin Jackson, aged 9, 'one of the children of the Widow Jackson'; John Champion and John Ffolkes, both aged 10; William Baldwin (a child of the Widow Baldwin), Richard Blomefield, and Thomas Bishop, whose ages are not given. And finally Robert Exham, aged about 7, not yet admitted, but to be so, on condition he came bearing two suits of clothes and a certificate to prove he had been born in Norwich.

The will of another Mayor, Robert Baron, which is dated 1649, left £250 to provide a separate Hospital for girls. In 1664 one was set up in Golden Dog Lane and two hundred years later a Girls' School of Housecraft (the one about which Janet Hitchman wrote)[1] was opened in Lakenham.

By 1742 according to the historian Blomefield there were thirty-six boys wearing the distinctive blue coats and red

[1] The King of the Barbareens

The Courtyard, Anguish's School, by P. E. Stimpson
1880–1948. After the school closed in 1885, the building
became a shoe factory. The school was demolished in the
1930s, the master's house in the 1960s.

caps of the Hospital in Fishergate. It continued as a boarding school until the early years of the nineteenth century, when it became a day-school. Finally in 1885 the school closed, the endowment money being used thereafter to help boys obtain secondary education or an apprenticeship. The building itself was sold and it became a shoe-factory.

It was this latter event that evoked a nostalgic response from a contributor to *The Norfolk and Norwich Annual* of 1887. He had been a 'bluebottle' attending the school at some unspecified date in the period when Dean Pellew was at the Cathedral (1828–1866). But his vagueness about dates is more than compensated for by his memory for visual detail. Here is his 'picture' of the Hospital building:- 'A "kidney"-paved quadrangle, flanked on three sides with stoutly constructed, low, 16th century buildings . . . here, a quaint old porch, the entrance to the Master's house; there, a penthouse-like, seated shelter for the boys; and on the other (fourth) side, a neatly-kept flower-and-kitchen garden, the pleasant resort of the Master after school hours which the scholars only surveyed through lofty palings'.

The schoolroom, our 'old boy' recalls, had an open-timbered, white-washed roof, and rows of fixed, closely-spaced desks 'with surfaces corrugated by the knives of schoolboys ambitious to have their names remembered'. These desks were arranged on either side of a central open space where the pupils were assembled in front of the Master's pulpit-desk.

Girls were also educated in the Fishergate school. 'Trim and neat', they wore a uniform consisting of a blue dress, white cross-over stomacher, black poke bonnet, long gloves and low shoes. The boys referred to the girls' hats as 'coalscuttles'. They themselves were arrayed in a distinctive uniform, the compulsory wearing of which taught them early how to defend themselves. Imagine a boy dressed in blue cloth trousers, a scarlet, black-speckled waistcoat, a short cutaway blue coat with brass buttons bearing the City Arms and, topping all, a flat, round, red worsted cap with blue bands and a blue woollen topknot. No wonder that many battles were fought with other youths on Castle Hill where the hurdles of the livestock-market acted as barricades.

On each Sunday morning during the school terms there was a church parade. The children had to attend this in full uniform, standing in a circle in the quadrangle of the Hospital while the register was called. Then, 'the massive oak gate was thrown open, and all marched away in procession to the Cathedral by way of Tabernacle Street'.

Our former 'bluebottle' cannot help but wonder why the children had to attend these services. It certainly was not that they might hear the Precentors, the Canon, Dean Pellew, or the preacher. For seated as they were, uncomfortably crushed together in the gallery (twixt organ and choir) no spoken word was audible. The music, on the other hand, was deafening. They took their own steps to make the tedium more bearable. Fruit and sweets were eaten surreptitiously by those whose 'seats' were the footrests of the children perched on the pews. Novels and adventure-stories were concealed inside prayer-books.

On two occasions in the year the school had to walk in procession to St. Edmund's Church instead of to the Cathedral. One of these occasions was the annual reading of the will of Thomas Anguish and of other later bequests to the school. How the ungrateful little beneficiaries apparently wriggled and sighed, wishing that the good Thomas had not been so wordy, and that the other benefactors had been fewer. But the other visit to St. Edmund's was even more of an ordeal for the youngters. For they knew that some of their number would be picked out by the clergyman to be publicly catechised. And not even the thought of the shilling 'reward' could make that prospect pleasing. The

philanthropic alderman who had initiated the gift little
knew the apprehension it would cause to succeeding generations of scholars.

The real highlights of the year for the children were the
two Scholars' Feasts, at Christmas and Easter. Our former
pupil recalled standing in the playground, looking into the
long kitchen beneath the school-room, where the tables
were set, and huge joints were turning slowly on their spits.
What excitement! What anticipation! And what a sense of
power when they finally sat down to eat and were waited
upon by the Master and his household.

For the relatives of the scholars quarter-day was important. It was then that they came to Fishergate to receive the
money allocated by the Trustees for the scholars' keep. This
of course was *not* what Thomas Anguish had intended. He
had wanted the children to be housed in the school. And had
the founder's wishes been adhered to, would the Hospital
School have survived beyond 1885? The writer of the article
in 'The Annual' thought this highly probable.

Sir Thomas Browne

Thomas Browne was not strictly speaking a 'son' of Norwich. He was born in London in 1605. His father, a merchant, died when Thomas was a child and his mother married Sir Thomas Dutton. Dutton appears to have filled the rôle both of kind father and good friend to his stepson, for in later years Thomas Browne spoke of having profited from the 'merciful disposition and humane inclination' of his parents. The boy received an excellent education, first at Wykeham's School, Winchester, then at Oxford where he gained a B.A. in 1626 and an M.A. in 1628. He practised medicine for a short while in Oxfordshire before leaving to travel extensively with his stepfather on the Continent. He continued his medical studies in Montpellier and Padua, and gained the degree of M.D. at Leyden in 1633. Between 1633 and 1636 he earned his living as a physician in Yorkshire, near Halifax, and it was during this period that he wrote his celebrated *Religio Medici*. This was circulated privately, in manuscript form, among his friends, some of whom copied it out.

In 1636 Browne moved south to Norwich at the exhortation of his former Oxford tutor and friend who had settled in the city the previous year. In 1641 he married Dorothy Mileham, a young lady from a well-established Norfolk family, and the following year Edward, the first of their

numerous family, was born. In 1642 also appeared the first
printed copies of *Religio Medici*. This had been produced,
without Browne's knowledge, by a London publisher, and
was such a success that it went into two editions. It contained so many errors, however, that Browne took the step
of authorizing a third edition corrected by himself. He was
to write more scholarly books, the most popular of which
were *Pseudo-doxia Epidemica* published in 1646 and *Urn
Burial* in 1658.

It was not only as a literary man that the Norwich
physician became renowned. He was regarded in his own
day as an authority in many different fields – natural history, archaeology, philosophy, and 'science' in general. His
specimen-room and herb gardens, one behind his house in
Orford Place, and one in the Lower Close, became included
in the 'sights' of the city. Through his scientific work and
interests he made friends in high places, men like John
Evelyn, the diarist. Partly because of this, partly because he
had remained loyal to the Royalist side throughout the Civil
War he was knighted by Charles II in 1671.

What of the man himself, the man behind the physician,
the scientist and the writer? In 1635 he wrote, 'No man truly
knows another . . . I am in the dark to all the world, and my
nearest friends behold me but in a cloud'. Even in this
statement he gives a glimpse of himself, and *Religio Medici* is
full of insights into Browne's character. It is a many-faceted
character – tolerant, superstitious, original, and disarming-
ly honest. Take his attitude, in that religiously troubled age,
to Roman Catholics. Although he states categorically that
'there is no Church whose every point is so square with my
conscience as the Church of England', he still claims that he
would happily worship in a Catholic church for want of an
Anglican one. He admits he can never hear 'an Ave Mary'
bell without 'an elevation', and points out that the Church
of England reformed *from* the Catholics, not *against* them.

Sir Thomas Browne. This famous Norwich citizen was buried in the church of St Peter Mancroft in 1682, where his memorial tablet can be seen. His statue, erected in 1905, stands on Hay Hill.

This breadth of vision no doubt derived from his long sojourns in Roman Catholic countries such as Italy and France. So too did his attitude to foreigners. Browne was a true 'European'. He hated to hear foreigners described by 'racist' epithets. 'By a word we wound thousands', he told his countrymen sternly. And he claimed to be 'at home' everywhere, whether eating frogs, snails and 'toadstools' (sic) with the French, or locusts and grasshoppers with the Jews.

His two 'Holy' books were the Bible and Nature. The world, as he saw it, was made to be inhabited by beasts but studied and contemplated by man. He would not admit of anything 'ugly' in Nature. Toads, bears and elephants were all equally to be wondered at as God's marvellous handiwork.

It is a shock to pass from such an educated 'modern' outlook to those passages in the book which deal with 'Angels' and 'Witches'. Browne suddenly recedes to a point far out of reach. He believed wholeheartedly in 'Guardian Angels' each with a 'charge' on earth, whom they might inspire to create a great work, or whom they might warn about an impending calamity. He believed just as implicitly in the reality of witches and this led him in 1664 into the one action which has remained a stain on his good name. He travelled to Bury St. Edmunds to give his learned opinion in a notorious witchcraft trial of two poor old women from Lowestoft who had been 'set up' by a gang of malicious locals. Children were produced to fake symptoms supposed to be the result of bewitching. Thomas Browne gave his opinion that the children had indeed been bewitched. 'I believe' he said in court, 'that the Devil, ever ready to work mischief, doth work upon the bodies of men and women upon a natural foundation.' Upon the testimony of such an eminent 'expert', the two old women were hanged.

Yet this is the same man who said, 'I cannot see a beggar

without relieving his necessities with my purse', and who could write with touching tenderness about his relationship with another man, 'I never yet cast a true appreciation on a woman, but I have loved my friend as I do virtue, my soul, my God . . . when I am from him, I am dead till I be with him; when I am with him, I am not satisfied, but would still be nearer him.'

This tenderness and capacity for loving never left Thomas Browne. It shines out, years later, in his many long letters to his children, particularly in those to his two eldest sons, Edward and Thomas. They had both been sent off at the age of fourteen to learn the customs of their European neighbours. Thomas had then joined the navy where he was to have a distinguished but tragically short career. At the beginning of 1667 he was Lieutenant on the *Marie Rose* which was at Portsmouth about to sail against the Dutch fleet. His father, having heard that another ship had blown itself up rather than be captured, had begun to worry that young Thomas and his Captain might think of following suit. 'I cannot omitt my earnest prayers unto God to deliver you from such a temptation,' he wrote earnestly, with much more in the same vein. He followed these exhortations with some commissions: 'When you are at Calais, see if you can get a box of the Jesuits' Powder at easier rate, & bring it in the bark, not in powder . . . Enquire further at Tangier of the minerall water you told mee, which was neere the towne and whereof made use. Take notice of such plants as you meet with either upon the Spanish or African coast; and if you knowe them not, putt some leaves into a booke, though carelessly, and not with that neatenesse as in your booke at Norwich'.

Edward had followed his father's profession and was eventually to become the King's Physician and the President of the Royal College of Surgeons. He was thirty-four years old when his father wrote to him about a rare French book on natural history which Edward had somehow acquired from the home of the Duke of Aylesbury. Thomas was highly excited about the acquisition and he bombarded Edward with instructions. The latter had to spend every spare moment transcribing the book and copying the woodcuts, lest he suddenly had to return it. He had to keep it away from rival naturalists, especially one, Moreland, who 'will drawe out of it for himself & his owne use, & so all the towne will take notice of it'. Thomas was agog to know what the woodcut of the elephant would look like, 'whether he bendeth his knees before and behind foreward, differently from other quadrupeds.' And he thought the book might contain 'the dissection of a camel . . . it was good to observe of what that bunch in the back consisteth.'

Then suddenly Browne, the elder, seems to bethink himself. He remembers who this son of his is, and how distinguished in his profession. 'I thought good to give you these hints,' he finished apologetically, 'because probably they would not come into your mind. . . . Your loving father etc.'

Thomas seems always to have remained a loving father, concerned about his family's welfare. In 1679 it was Edward's health that worried him. 'Extraordinarie sickly seasons wearie physicians and robb them of their health as well as their quiet; have therefore a great care of your health . . . (by) temperance, and sobrietie, and a good competence of sleep,' he advised. 'Take heed the Tobacco gayne not too much upon you, for the great incomodities that may ensue . . . the hart burning after much taking at a time, and also the impayring of the memorie. . . .'

His own heart stopped on 10th October 1682 which happened to be his birthday. It is said that he had contracted a chill four days earlier when he went out on a late call. In his *Christian Morals*, which was published posthumously, Sir Thomas Browne had written, 'Reckon not upon long Life;

think every day the last, and live always beyond thy account. He that so often survivith his Expectation lives many Lives, and will scarce complain of the shortness of his days.'

It might have been his epitaph.

The Sufferings of the Quakers

To understand why there were Quaker persecutions at all, we need to look briefly at the history of the sect. The founder of the movement, George Fox, was a visionary young countryman from Leicestershire. He was eighteen years old when the Civil War broke out in 1642. The country was in a ferment at that time both politically and religiously. The lad, Fox, looked around him and was profoundly disillusioned. On the one side he found corrupt High Churchmen, on the other hypocritical Puritan preachers. In 1643 he left his home and his shoemaking apprenticeship and, like many others in that age, he became a 'traveller'. For years he wandered the countryside, meeting up with different religious groups, exchanging ideas with them, then continuing on his quest. By 1647, at twenty-three years of age, he had worked out a doctrine and a way of life which he found completely fulfilling. Basically it was a return to pure, primitive Christianity without parish church, priest, sacrament, or liturgy. These, to Fox, were shadows that blotted out the light of God. Fox believed that every human being had the divine potential to become Christ-like without any earthly mediator. Christianity was to him a living force. This 'blasphemy' he now began to preach to others, and soon suffered imprisonment because of it.

But it was the financial and political aspects of Fox's doctrine that really troubled the authorities of the day. Because the Quakers did not attend their parish-churches they refused to pay church-rates, or 'tithes'. That was bad enough. On top of it Fox had the temerity to suggest that the revenues of the Established Church and of the great nobles of the land ought to be distributed to help the poor. This was dangerous radicalism, even in the eyes of the Cromwellian government. The Quakers' behaviour in fact was generally disruptive. Not only did they think they had the right to stand up in church and contradict the preachers, but they would not remove their hats to the magistrates in court. They maintained that they could not doff their hat to a 'superior', because every man was born equal. The same reasoning forbade them to use the respectful 'you' to their so-called 'superior', rather than the familiar 'thou'. Finally, most infuriating of all to officialdom, no Quaker would swear an oath. This was one of their strictest tenets. They explained that they were obeying Christ's commandment to 'swear not at all', and if they were to swear an oath in particular circumstances this would infer that normally they did not speak the truth.

These were the troublemakers, most of them hardly more than boys and girls, who came to Norwich as missionaries in the 1650s. They harassed the City Fathers and they gave the louts an excuse for indulging in violence. George Whitehead, a nineteen-year-old schoolteacher, arrived in the city in 1654. He attended a service in the church of St. Peter Mancroft where he stood up to question the preacher. He was almost torn in two by the congregation before being hauled across the market place to the Guildhall to appear before the Mayor, Thomas Toft. The Mayor had him thrown into the Castle gaol where Whitehead spent most of the subsequent winter sleeping on bare floorboards in a cold room.

By the spring of 1655 there were quite a few converts in the city. In his *Autobiography* George Whitehead tells how his friend and landlord, John Lawrence, was summoned to appear before the Independent Congregation of St. George's, Tombland. George Whitehead accompanied him to give him moral support. So too did Lawrence's brother-in-law, Edmund Bedwell. Unfortunately Bedwell felt it necessary to wear his sword. Whitehead saw this as a mistake, but whether it increased the antagonism of the congregation is doubtful. It was against young Whitehead, the 'foreigner' who had led Lawrence astray, that their hostility was directed. As soon as he stood up to speak in Lawrence's defence, the women set about him. Their men-folk were not long in joining in. The young man was hauled out of the church and along the streets to the market-place. He was thrown roughly down on the stones so many times that he was soon in considerable pain from his bruises. Did they intend to pillory him in the market-place in front of the Guildhall? Probably. But Whitehead managed to break away. He ran along St. Giles Street, 'until I came near to the City-Gate called Giles's Gate, next to a little Pasture-Ground', he writes, 'and at the upper end whereof I saw a great House where the Lady Hubbard dwelt'. He ran towards the house hoping for sanctuary, 'the tumultuous, raging company continuing still about me'. The noise brought some members of the family and Lady Hubbard's chaplain to the door. If Whitehead had hoped for assistance he was to be disappointed. The chaplain began to taunt him, asking why, if he were possessed of the same Spirit as the Apostles, Whitehead could not pacify the mob. It was one of Cromwell's armed troopers chancing on the scene some-time later who came to the young Quaker's rescue and escorted him back to John Lawrence's house.

These early Quakers had of necessity to meet for worship in private houses. In the last week of May 1660, the very

St Giles Gate 1792. There was a leper-house just outside it from the 14th century until at least 1604.

week, when Charles II landed at Dover, the Norwich Quakers were assembled in the house of Joseph Whitlock in St. Edmund's parish (the Fishergate – Whitefriars area) for Sunday worship. In a letter of bitter complaint to the Mayor, they described how their meeting had been invaded by a band of local louts. They named the ringleaders as 'Christopher Benet, apprentice to Zachariah Mayhew of St. Augustine's; John Sadler of St. Paul's; John Sammon a servant at the Brewhouse without Pockthorp Gates'. As they were accustomed to being disturbed the Quakers had taken the precaution of locking and bolting both an outer and an inner gate, and two doors. All these were broken down and forty foot of window glass was smashed by stones. Once inside, the three ringleaders encouraged their mob to set about the Quakers themselves: 'smiting, punching, pulling some of us by the arms to hale us out of the Meeting . . . pushing us from one to another and dragging us about . . . dragging some by the hair and spitting in their faces . . . drawing of blood, throwing of fire . . . several of them getting on the table and throwing themselves violently down upon the heads of men and women . . . some of them holding the maid of the house whilst others daubed her face with gore and dung, so that the skin of her face could hardly be seen'.

The letter of complaint took the Quaker who bore it to confinement in the Castle Gaol for some trumped-up offence. Benet, Sadler, and Sammon were never charged.

After the Restoration of Charles II it seemed for a short time as though the position of the Quakers would improve. The King was personally sympathetic towards them, and when he officially declared liberty of conscience to all who kept the peace, this included Quakers. Those who were really in charge of the country were nervously watching for any sign of insurrection. To them the Quakers were a dangerously disruptive element. So, when in January 1661, a small band of fanatics called the Fifth Monarchy Men staged an abortive uprising the Quakers, who had no connection with them, suffered. They were now categorically forbidden to meet together for worship. When they ignored this edict, 4230 of them – men, women, and children – were thrown into prison.

George Whitehead found himself once again in Norwich Castle Gaol that January. 'We were so crowded in the Castle,' he recalled in his *Autobiography*, 'that we had not convenient room for Lodging, about thirty or above being then crowded in that old, nasty prison, and there being a Hole in the corner of the Castle Wall called the 'Vice', we four friends betook ourselves (there), though a poor narrow Hole without any Chimney in it . . . we got up two little beds and lodged two in each . . . but having an old decayed stone arch over it, the rain came so much in upon us, that we could not well keep it off our beds, though we set dishes or basons to keep off what we could'. When the winter evenings were very cold they suffered the fumes and smoke of a small charcoal fire in the chimney-less room. In the daytime they found another way to keep themselves warm. . . . 'by walking upon the Castle-hill and under the wall, being within the Liberty of the prison; 'twas but a cold, bleak place in winter, yet we were glad that we had that benefit of air'.

In February 1661 there was another raid on the house of Joseph Whitlock of St. Edmund's, this time by officials. Alderman Augustine Briggs descended on the Meeting to serve the Mayor's warrant. The men were then taken to the house of the Mayor, Joseph Paine. There they had to sit in the courtyard while the Mayor finished his dinner. When they were finally taken into the hall they found the Recorder, Francis Cory, one of their chief persecutors in the city, sitting there too. They were ordered to take the Oath of Allegiance to the King which they all refused to do. Was it because Joseph Paine had himself suffered imprisonment, for his royalist sympathies, that his behaviour towards the Quakers was less harsh than that of other officials? At any rate he seemed reluctant to dispatch them to jail. He told the poor among them to think of their wives and children and he made a particular effort to save one young Quaker, Samuel Duncan, from imprisonment. Samuel was still serving an apprenticeship, and his master's nephew was apparently in the company that had been dining with Paine. This gentleman was quick to speak up for Samuel. 'He is a faithful Prentice although he be of this persuasion,' he told the Mayor. The Mayor called upon a clergyman, Dr. Starky, another of the company, to take Samuel Duncan into the garden and try to talk some sense into him. Their well-meaning efforts were of no avail. Young Samuel was true to his creed. In due course, with eight companions, he was led off to the miserable dungeon beneath the Guildhall.

Throughout the 1660s one Act after another was passed against Quakers, each more severe than the last. The most pernicious Act of all was passed in 1670. This was the Second Conventicle Act whereby informers were rewarded for reporting Quaker assemblies and giving the names of their preachers. In July 1670 the informers Richard Wright and Nicholas Spendlove reported to Alderman Henry Herne, of the Over-the-Water ward, that there was a Quakers' meeting at the house of Ann Whitlock, widow of Joseph. When the officers led the Quakers out into the street the hostility of the watching crowd seems to have been directed on this occasion against the informers. The Quakers could not win, however. In addition to the other charges brought against them they were accused of having caused a riot by pointing out the informers to the mob.

Between 1672 and 1682 Norwich Quakers suffered mainly through having their goods withheld for non-payment of

tithes. Besse[1] supplies a particularly vivid account of how
the wife of Samuel Duncan was treated by the parish
officers of St. Gregory's one July week-end in 1678. Mistress Duncan, far advanced in pregnancy, was looking after
the shop on the Saturday evening because her husband was
away on business. As William Poole, the parish constable,
passed by he saw that the shop-door was open. This was
obviously an opportunity for which he had been waiting,
for he hastened to tell the news to John Crowe the church-
warden, who was an attorney by profession. So eager
was Crowe to get into the Duncans' shop that he left his
dinner. Once arrived there he pretended he had come to see
Samuel, then he kept Mistress Duncan talking until John
Poole returned with Edward Mayhew, one of the parish
overseers. The three men proceeded to take over the shop,
making it plain that they were going to remain there until
Monday, when they would be able to move out the dis-
trained goods. That night the maid locked the door between
the shop and the family living-rooms, but on Sunday
morning she found the lock broken and the men in the inner
rooms.

To begin with poor Mistress Duncan was allowed neither
to go out or have any visitors. In view of her condition the
magistrates quickly saw that this situation did not continue.
Local feeling must obviously have been stirred up on her
account too, for John Crowe is reported to have said
fearfully 'We shall have our throats cut'. Perhaps it was this
likelihood that took him back to his own home on Sunday
night to get some sleep. He returned promptly enough on
Monday morning and shut up the shop windows which had
been opened for business. Then he assembled his crew of
removal men. This comprised, in addition to the three
parish-officers who had slept in the shop, Gamaliel Sugden;

[1] An Account of the Sufferings of the People called Quakers

Thomas Southgate junior, the second overseer; Charles
Teneson, an informer; Thomas Gideons, a carter; Thomas
Woods, John Browne, and Robert Phoebe, helpers; and 'the
Hangman' who said he was sent to help them by his master,
Francis Bacon, Steward. They proceeded to strip the shop
and house even to the 'boards that were fit for (i.e. fitted to)
the doors to keep little children in'. They had difficulty in
finding a hammer because none of the neighbours would
lend them one. The Hangman finally borrowed one from
Charles Aldman, a vintner, who came along to give
encouragement, though he later denied this.

The 'rude rabble' still gave the Quakers trouble whenever
there was an opportunity. On Christmas Day 1676 when
the Quakers refused to close their shops both Jane Bangs
and Samuel Duncan had snowballs and bones thrown in at
their doors. When 'some sober people passing said (to the
hooligans) they would be sent to Bridewell . . . they
replied, *they* might as well be sent to Bridewell for
complaining'.

The most terrible period of persecution was still to come
between 1682 and 1685. This persecution was part of the
hysterical reaction against Whiggery and, in particular, the
Rye House Plot to murder King Charles and his brother,
James. Quakers in London, Bristol, and Norwich suffered
more severe and continuous harassment than they had ever
done before. The letters they wrote appealing for justice,
and describing their maltreatment can still shock and appal,
even when read in the serene atmosphere of the County
Record Office. 'We are men who have lived well and
comfortably in our trades,' one of the prisoners stated
poignantly in a letter to Justice Freeman. Another appeal
directed at the Mayor and Alderman of the city pointed out
that several of them were employers of many hundreds of
combers, spinners, and knitters, 'and some of us have not
anyone we can trust that is capable to manage our business'.

The horrific conditions under which they were existing were detailed in a letter by Edward Monk written in the spring of 1683 to the Judges of the Assize at Thetford. Twenty-four Quakers and six criminals were crammed into one 'hole'. Nine men were in a musty dungeon, twenty-seven steps into the ground, with neither chimney nor 'place of easement', and with the small window sometimes locked up so that they were almost stifled. Nine women were in a little close cellar without a chimney. In the meanwhile rooms in the jail lay empty, rooms for which the Quakers could not, or would not, pay the exorbitant fees demanded by the gaoler.

It was 1685 before there was any amelioration in the Quakers' position. A General Pardon, really aimed at Roman Catholics, released them from their terrible prisons. In 1689 Dutch William came to the English throne and the Toleration Act permitted freedom of worship to protestant nonconformists. In February 1699 Norwich Quakers opened their New Meeting House in the Gildencroft beside the burial-ground which they had purchased twenty-seven years earlier. Parts only of this building are incorporated in the meeting-house we see there today, for most of it was destroyed in an air-raid in April 1942. Here are perpetuated the memories of Norwich's later Quaker families who contributed so much to the city both materially and intellectually. But these – the Gurneys, the Barclays, and the Aldersons – were the inheritors of a legacy that had been won with much suffering, by those early Friends incarcerated in their grim dungeons. Gildencroft Meeting-House is primarily their memorial.

Prideaux' City

Dr. Humphrey Prideaux came to Norwich in 1686 to be a Prebendary of the Cathedral. He was a Cornishman, thirty-eight years old, and an academic of some note. He had taken his degree at Oxford and had remained there for another eighteen years in a variety of posts. By 1686 he and the Oxford hierarchy no longer saw eye to eye. It was thanks to the Lord Chancellor's patronage that Prideaux got the Norwich post and was able to move.

Until 1694 Prideaux divided his time between Norwich and Saham Toney, whose rector he had become in 1686. In 1694 he decided to transfer his family to Norwich for the sake of their health. All of them, Dr. Prideaux included, had been plagued by constant sickness while they lived at Saham. The ague in particular had afflicted them and two of his children had become so debilitated because of it that they were never to recover. Through Prideaux' letters to his friend John Ellis, published by the Camden Society in 1875, we see late 17th Century Norwich from the viewpoint of a staunchly Protestant churchman who did not suffer either fools or villains gladly.

Prideaux was a conscientious, hard-working man for whom the post of Prebendary was no sinecure. When he first arrived in Norwich he found the affairs of the Cathedral in great disarray. On the financial side no 'books' had been kept for years. The priceless archives of the place lay on bare earth in a room with broken windows. Prideaux restored order with files, catalogues, and account-books. He also saw that the fabric of the Cathedral was inspected annually and repaired when necessary. When he returned to live in the Close in 1694 he was again faced with the running of the Cathedral. This was mainly because of the shortcomings of Dean Fairfax. Fairfax was Prideaux' 'cross' for many years, and one which he did not bear gladly.

'I am now at Norwich, where the Dean behaves himselfe more like a beast than ever, and is so obstinate and perverse in his own humours which are indeed intolerable, that there is no endureing of him,' he wrote to Ellis in November 1693.

The following month he was even more dispirited. 'We are here at a miserable passe with this horrid sot we have got for our Dean,' he complained. 'He cannot sleep at night till dosed with drink.' Even worse, as Prideaux explained, was that the Dean always insisted his manservant join him in his carousing. And since he sacked his servants regularly, they spread tales about him all over the county. Indeed one of Fairfax's former servants was currently butler to a country gentleman called Earle 'a drinking, loud gentleman' and the latter had the butler entertain his guests with scandalous stories about the old Dean.

It was not only the Dean's drunkenness that annoyed his colleagues. He knew nothing of 'justice, honesty, civility, or good manners'. He seldom went to church. He never took Holy Communion. He did not open a book from one year's end to another. 'Goe to him when you will,' Prideaux told Ellis, 'you will find him walking about his roome with a pipe in his mouth and a bottle of claret and a bottle of old strong beer . . . upon the table, and every other turn he takes a glass of one or the other of them.'

So much for life inside the Close, that Close which

Prideaux described as 'a town of itselfe, apart from the city, separated from it by walls and gates'. He claimed to have little to do with the folk outside the Close walls: 'I take care to have nothing at any time to doe with them except in my profession'. Nevertheless he knew of every storm in the teacup of civic affairs and took a lively interest in them. One of these blew up in April 1696 as a result of a crisis in central government.

After the death of Queen Mary (Stuart) in 1692, William III's popularity waned. He was a 'foreigner' after all. He had made enemies amongst both Tories and Whigs in Parliament and a sizeable section of the populace had Jacobite sympathies and were hoping for James II's return from exile. Under these circumstances the discovery of an assassination-plot in February 1696, the 'Turnham Green Plot', seriously alarmed the government. The King's subjects must demonstrate their loyalty, they decided. Each corporate body was to sign a form which said, 'In case His Majesty come to any violent or untimely death, we do . . . oblige ourselves to unite, associate, and stand by each other in revenging the same upon his enemies and their adherents'.

The Norwich City Fathers were a cautious bunch. They still had unpleasant memories of the riots that had occurred in the city in November 1689 when news was received that the Prince of Orange had landed in England. The 'Mob' had first attacked and plundered the houses of Roman Catholics, then had progressed to indiscriminate pillaging, and violence. Indeed had it not been for Dr. Prideaux' foresight in locking the gates to the Close, a crowd five-hundred strong would have invaded the houses of the clergy, and probably the Cathedral church. So when it was moved at a meeting by Alderman Robert Cooke that the word 'revenging', being too inflammatory, should be replaced by 'punishing' the motion was carried.

Humphrey Prideaux. Described in the Dictionary of
National Biography as an orientalist, distinguished for
his scholarship, whose letters to his friend Ellis, 'exhibit
him as a man of more frankness than refinement of
mind'.

According to Prideaux, Robert Cooke was the wealthiest
man in the city. He was a non-conformist and a cloth-
manufacturer. So it was somewhat ironic that it should be
the Society of Weavers who took exception to the corporation's decision to delete the word 'revenging', and who
decided to retain it in a separate declaration of their own. Sir
Henry Hobart, of the anti-Stuart faction, apparently put
them up to it and it was generally believed that the weavers
were currying favour with the government so that their Bill
for prohibiting the import of Indian silks would be carried.

Whatever the reason for the weavers causing this schism
Norwich was soon in the headlines because of it. A political
news-sheet called *The Postboy*, printed in London, published a defamatory article about Norwich's Mayor and
aldermen, virtually accusing them of treason. The article
even suggested that Dr. Prideaux had played a part in the
business. 'Every word is false,' he told Ellis angrily. The
Mayor responded by sending the Town Clerk up to London to threaten the editor of *The Postboy* with a libel action
unless he divulged his source of 'information'. This he
obviously did, for in a letter dated 17th April, Prideaux
refers to 'the slur about the Association made by the
Weavers and their correspondent, the writer of *The Postboy*.' We do not hear what were the consequences of the
revelation, only that the city had to celebrate the ensuing
Day of Thanksgiving with excessive zeal to show they were
no traitors.

Dr. Prideaux was obviously nervous of the Jacobite
element in Norwich. He gave constant reports to his friend,
Ellis, about Jacobites and their misdeeds. In July 1692 a
couple of them had been overheard by a chimney-sweep
who had been having a nap beside Harford Bridge. They
had just returned from the Continent and were discussing
how James would be back on the throne before the harvest
was in. When they spied the eavesdropper, one of the

Jacobites would have shot him. The other, however, was more civilised. He prevailed upon his mate just to tie the man up, so that he could not follow them. They left him by the side of the road where he was found by a cart-driver and taken to Norwich. He went to the Mayor and testified to what he had overheard.

A Norwich physician called Bambridge was viewed by Prideaux with great suspicion. He could not have earned more than £40 a year from his practice, yet he lived at the rate of £400 per annum. No-one knew where he got his money, but he was very friendly with the Duke of Norfolk. 'I have suspected him these ten years to be a spy,' Prideaux declared in 1696.

The Archbishop of Glasgow was 'skulking' in Norwich in July 1696, Prideaux told Ellis, and the principal Jacobites were meeting him covertly. A local Jacobite who did not skulk but met his like-minded friends quite openly was Sir Robert Yallup of Bowthorpe, 'a very turbulent, enter-priseing knave'. In 1695 he and his coterie had met regularly at the Goat tavern on Saturday afternoons hiring a private room from four in the afternoon until nine o'clock at night. They were eventually forbidden their meetings by the city authorities.

In June 1697 Prideaux told how a group of Jacobites, who had been celebrating the birthday of the Prince of Wales, had come to grief. They had all become drunk and on their way home from the tavern Doedale, an Irishman, quar-relled with his friend, Captain Ogilby, a Scotsman. The latter was another 'skulking' Jacobite who had been living with a local widow. Doedale ran Ogilby through, killing him. The murderer fled, so the authorities arrested his companions who had also drawn their swords during the brawl. 'The Jacobites here grow higher than ever . . . This will cut their combes a little', commented Prideaux with small charity.

He had little charity too for those malefactors who in
1696 were confined in the smallpox stricken Castle Gaol.
On 10th April he told Ellis how seven prisoners had been
sentenced to death at the Assizes, four for burglary, two for
highway-robbery, and one for clipping coins. Several prisoners had been discharged 'by an over-kind jury'. And there
were some who could not be tried because they had small-
pox. 'It would have been a very bloody assizes, had all had
sentence of death that deserved it,' he observed. As regards
the condemned men, it was the state of their souls rather
than their fate that concerned Prideaux: 'They are stout
fellows all of them, but as hardened criminals as ever I heard
of in my life. . . . those few minutes they have left, they
spend in the height of leudness and frolick.' If this is
reminiscent of *The Beggar's Opera*, even more so were the
scenes enacted at the gaol a few days later.

The seven accused men were to be hanged on 17th April
and their coffins were delivered to them by friends a few
days before the fatal date. How it was engineered Prideaux
does not tell, but at some stage the coffins had been filled
with arms, tools, and provisions. The seven freed themselves from their irons. Their attempt at a break-out failed
so they took possession of the dungeon (the only entrance to
which was a narrow passage) and held it until 17th April.
On that morning soldiers who were quartered in the city
were brought in to break the siege. As they stormed the
dungeon one of the accused swallowed poison. Oil was
immediately poured down the poor wretch's throat to
make him vomit for the hangman was not to be cheated out
of a victim. 'They were seven desperate sturdy villains and
we are well rid of them. When they came to the gallows,
they did lament that they had been deceived by some at
London who fed them with promises of pardon,' Prideaux
concluded.

At the other end of the social scale the Duke of Norfolk

and his friends came in for much censure from Prideaux.
On 24th August 1696 he told Ellis, 'The Duke of Norfolk
brought down one Mrs. Love, his mistress, with him, who
made a great show here; but failed in his main aim – to
entertain himself with the ladys . . . when he had made
preparations for a ball, none would come to it.' In December 1699 it was some other friends of the Duke upon whom
Prideaux was frowning: 'The Duke of Norfolk hath been
here; and some will have it that his only business was to fix
Dogget and his Players here, who have now their stage up at
the Duke's place, and are helping all they can to undoe this
place, which, on the decay of their weaveing trade, now
sinks apace. But I suppose His Grace had some other design
in this journey than for the sake of those varletts'.

Thomas Doggett was the young Irish actor-manager
who was to become manager of Drury Lane Theatre. This
was the decade of the exuberant satirical comedies of Congreve and Vanbrugh which seem harmless enough today.
Dr. Prideaux was not alone in his disapproval of 'those
varletts' to whom the Duke was Patron. In 1698 Jeremy
Collier, the clergyman outlawed in 1696 for publicly
absolving the King's would-be assassins on the scaffold,
published *A Short View of the Immorality and Profaneness of the
English Stage* in which he castigated the contemporary
theatre for profanity of language and the current trend for
mocking the clergy on the stage. The pamphlet was extremely influential and resulted in several prosecutions of
playwrights, Congreve among them.

In June 1702 on the death of the troublesome Fairfax,
Prideaux became Dean of Norwich, a just reward for years
of conscientious service. Unhappily 'after years of pain' an
operation for 'the stone' which he underwent in 1712 went
catastrophically wrong. From then until his death in 1724 he
suffered constant pain and a variety of bodily infirmities. In
a letter to a cousin, written in his seventy-first year, Dean

Prideaux explained how matters were with him: 'If I outlive the ensuing winter, it is more than I expect or indeed desire: for I have now upon me those decays both of body and mind as make me fully sensible, "*Gravis est et dura senectus*".'

The Scots Society

The Scots Society came into being on St. Andrew's Day 1774. An assembly of exiled Scots had been celebrating the festival of their patron saint with some enthusiasm. At the end of the proceedings they found they had a surplus of three shillings and sixpence and one of the company suggested it be laid aside as a kind of 'distress fund'. Another ten shillings was immediately contributed and it was formally announced that the fund would be at the disposal of 'any poor Scotsman who might come to Norwich in distress and might need the whole or any part of it.'

At this date any Scot (or other 'foreigner') who found himself destitute in England was in a sorry plight. The various local Poor Law bodies found it difficult enough to support their own poor, and would rarely provide assistance for outsiders. Private charity, too, tended to begin and end at home. Thus the rich merchants and clothiers of Norwich might dig into their pockets to help unfortunate fellow-citizens, but would invariably give a penurious stranger the cold shoulder.

On 30th November 1775 the Scottish gentlemen who assembled in Norwich again on St. Andrew's Day found themselves with an embarrassment of riches. Not only had the 'emergency fund' of thirteen shillings and sixpence not yet been drawn upon, but it had grown to three pounds. It was decided that the handling of the fund must be put upon a proper basis. Not very speedily, but with Scottish thoroughness, the matter was taken in hand. In 1776 the Scots Society was officially formed, full membership being restricted to Scots, and associate membership offered to Englishmen. By 1777 the first committee had been elected. The Earl of Rosebery was Governor, Dr. John Murray was President, Mr. John Dalrymple was Steward, and Messrs. John and Bartlett Gurney were the Society's bankers. At this point it was resolved that the Society's funds should be used to help strangers in general, and not just Scots.

As it turned out the first recipient of the Society's charity was a Scotsman, Alexander Geddes, who in 1778 was 'ill of a putrid fever' and in great difficulties. Geddes eventually recovered, but his case had obviously given the committee food for thought. It was decided that should one of their protégés die without heirs their possessions should come to the Society. There was apparently no objection to this resolution though the legality of it seems a shade doubtful. The Society's official seal was donated to it in this year by a Mr. Cairnes of Birmingham. It showed St. Andrew on his cross, and beneath him, the words, 'Love Ye The Stranger'. By St. Andrew's Day, 1778, five Scotsmen had been assisted out of the fund, and two had been buried at the Society's expense.

As the committee found its feet other wrinkles in the running of the Society were ironed out. Agents were appointed in outlying towns to deal with distressed strangers who could not travel to Norwich. In order to ensure that their protégés received proper medical care, an annual subscription of two guineas was paid to the recently built Norfolk and Norwich Hospital. The city workhouses agreed to accept 'cases' from the Society on condition that they were paid two shillings a week for each individual's board and lodging.

We are fortunate in having a contemporary description of both these institutions, with which the Scots Society liaised. Maximilien de Lazowski, tutor to the young Count of La Rochefoucauld, wrote about them in 1784[1]. He was enthusiastic about the hospital: 'Nothing could be cleaner or simpler: there is no finery or show, only comfort and good care and scrupulous cleanliness. It is intended for a hundred people, half of them men, half women. . . . The sick are kept in large, well-aired rooms provided with ventilators, the bedsteads are of iron and the curtains of linen so that they may be washed as often as need be. . . . The infirmary stands outside the walls of the old town, with a lot of land adjoining, enough for pasture and fodder for some cows and for a horse if needed for service. . . . I never in my life saw an infirmary so clean, so well managed with so little means, in which there is no more odour than there is in the house of an individual who cares about cleanliness'.

In the workhouse, unfortunately, the odour was more noticeable. Lazowski blamed the age and condition of the building for the 'perpetual stench'. He had to admit, however, that 'The poor are well looked after and clothed according to their needs . . . they are well-nourished, eating three times a day, with meat three times a week; on the other four days, milk products and vegetables; there are two meals a day when they have only butter or cheese, but at all meals and every day they have small beer'.

Not all the applicants to the Scots Society were looking for money to help them survive. Robert Randal, a Scottish highwayman in Norwich Castle, was concerned that after his execution he might not receive a decent burial. In view of the fact that he had shown remorse for his crime and behaved with propriety since his arrest it was resolved

[1] *A Frenchman's Year in Suffolk: 1784*. Edited and translated by Norman Scarfe.

that seventeen shillings should be awarded 'towards the interment of that unhappy man.'

Nor were all the Society's recipients temporary residents in the locality. In 1785 the family of Solomon Jacob, a Jewish resident of Norwich, but one who had no legal 'settlement' there, either through birth or his trade, was in dire straits. Through no fault of Jacob's he had fallen behind with his rent. As a result his home had been literally stripped bare by his landlord. The family were starving and lying on bare boards when Bishop Bagot 'a mild and amiable gentleman', the historian Jessup calls him, heard of their plight. He and other subscribers to the Scots Society recommended that the Jacob family receive help. Five pounds worth of furniture was bought for them and from then on the Jacobs were taken under the Society's wing and helped in times of sickness and 'lyings-in'.

On one of the coldest days of that same winter of 1784–5 a man who claimed to be German, but who was called Lewis Le Febure, was found 'in a perishing condition' on Cawston Moor ten miles from Norwich. He was taken in and restored to health by the humane poor-law officers of a nearby parish, after which a local J.P. referred him to the Scots Society in Norwich. The man had been with the German troops who had fought on the English side in the American War of Independence. When hostilities ceased, he was shipped back to Hull, where his troop was disbanded. He had been given what was deemed sufficient money to take him to Great Yarmouth, whence he could get a passage to Germany. But he had fallen ill, and having managed to make his way as far as Cawston Heath, had finally collapsed, worn out with fatigue and hunger. He was given sufficient money to continue his journey home.

In November 1785 it was decided to change the Society's name. No longer would it be the Scots Society. From now on it was the Society of Universal Goodwill. Bishop Bagot

St Andrew's Hall. This 15th century church of the Black
Friars was sold to the city at the Dissolution. The nave
became today's St Andrew's Hall and the choir the
present Blackfriars Hall.

was invited to fill the office of Guardian, which he willingly did. It was also resolved, 'that all Societies bearing the same name as this, in any part of the world, shall be considered as one body, correspond and carry on a friendly intercourse with each other'.

In 1786 John Edwards, aged twenty-four, a native of Pennsylvania was found hiding in a barn near Wolterton Hall, the home of Lord Walpole. Since Lord Walpole was the local J.P., Edwards was brought before him. By the man's own account he was another 'casualty' of war. He had served in the British Navy until 1783 when the Peace of Versailles put an end to the American war. No longer a British subject he was discharged from the service and turned loose in London. Having worked on the land as a boy he began to travel round the countryside looking for farmwork. He had managed to feed himself in this way for some time, but finally his luck ran out. Exhausted and starving he had crept into the barn to die.

Lord Walpole saw to it that the man was fed. Not knowing what to do with him he sent him to Aylsham Bridewell. When the justices next sat there an order was made to remove Edwards to Norwich Castle gaol. The man claimed that he now wished to return to America so Lord Walpole recommended that he be referred to the Society of Universal Goodwill. The Society gave Edwards some decent clothing, he was almost naked, sufficient money to take him to London and a letter to the American ambassador asking that the man be allowed to sail home in the first vessel bound for Philadelphia. Lord Walpole was obviously so impressed by this that he became a regular subscriber to the Society who in that year had helped 335 individuals out of difficulties.

That the committee were sometimes willing to 'bend the rules' if necessary is seen in the story of the Widow Kelson. Her husband, William Kelson, had been a 'fireworker' in the iron foundry of Messrs Bartlett Gurney and Robert Ransome in Norwich. Kelson had always let it be known that he had been born at sea, and had never qualified, either through apprenticeship or work, for a 'settlement' any-where in England. This meant that when he was sick and unable to work he received no dole from the Norwich authorities. The Society of Universal Goodwill came to the widow's assistance shortly after Kelson's death. On the recommendation of the Mayor and of Mr. Richard Gurney she was awarded a weekly allowance of six shillings to keep her two children. In due time it was discovered that the late William Kelson had been born in a village near Bath. So by rights his widow and children should have been handed over to the Norwich Poor Law authorities to be transported to Bath. Enquiries being made the Widow Kelson was found to be a particularly industrious and enterprising lady. With the help of her twelve-year-old step-daughter she was running quite a thriving tailoring business and keeping her family and home 'in an easy, decent, and comfortable manner'. The six-shilling allowance from the Society was being used to educate 'a promising boy of about six years old'.

Why then, the committee asked, should they have this 'industrious good woman and two friendless orphans de-ported?' It was hardly *their* fault that William Kelson had given false information. They were living peacefully at the moment in a neighbourhood where they were well-known and where the widow had many connections. It was re-solved in the end that the Society should become temporary Guardians to the family, gradually decreasing their dole as the requirements grew less.

There were rogues and fraudsters to be reckoned with. 'Major' Mackenzie was one of these. He arrived in Norwich in the summer of 1787 and whatever he lacked it was certainly not imagination. Had Mackenzie written down his 'life-story', which he related to Dr. Murray and many others, he might have beaten Walter Scott to the gun and become the first great romantic Scottish novelist.

According to the Major, his father had been a certain Colonel Mackenzie who, in his youth, had emigrated from Scotland to Hungary to join the army of the Austrian Emperor. He had become a Roman Catholic and had married a rich Hungarian heiress thus acquiring a vast estate. On part of this estate he had founded a small monastery. The Major had been the only son of the union and had been destined from the outset for a military career. He had risen early to the rank of major but then, alas, had become involved in a quarrel and a disastrous duel with his Lieutenant-Colonel. Having killed the latter, he and his wife had to flee the country. They sought refuge in Ireland where, for a while, the Major was liberally supported by his father. He then became convinced of the errors of the Church of Rome and left the Catholic Church. He had a certificate signed by the Bishop of Cork to attest to his recantation. His father consequently disinherited him and, egged on by the monks, had the Major excommunicated 'in a most solemn manner'.

At this point Fate took a hand in exacerbating the Major's predicament. Mrs. Mackenzie, hitherto 'barren', suddenly began producing offspring. The family's debts mounted. They fled from Ireland to England where, owing to the spite of an Irish priest, they were imprisoned in Newgate. Somehow the Major's well-connected Scottish relatives heard of his plight. They bought the family out of prison, before apparently vanishing into thin air. But there was a faint gleam of hope in the hitherto dark heavens. The Major had received a pardon from the Austrian Emperor. He had a certificate signed 'Joseph' to prove it. He could return home now with his family, if only. . . .

Dr. Murray, president of the Society of Universal Goodwill, smelled a rat. He wrote to the Imperial Ambassador to ask if he could verify Mackenzie's story. There was a long delay occasioned by the fact that a new ambassador had recently taken office. Dr. Murray had to write a second letter of enquiry. Meanwhile the Major was gathering in contributions from the gullible to help him on his way. Finally, at the end of September, the long-awaited reply arrived from the Comte de Revviczky. He had never heard of either Colonel or Major Mackenzie. After all, he gently pointed out, 'le nom de Mackenzie n'est certainement pas Hongrois'.

When the Major heard what Dr. Murray had been up to, he made an appropriately theatrical exit, hiring a carriage, and eloping with an unnamed young lady of fourteen years. Both carriage and damsel were recovered the following day at Aylsham, but Mackenzie escaped. The Mayor had posters circulated asking for information about his whereabouts. Some time later the Marquis of Townshend heard a story suggesting that Mackenzie was now operating his fraudulent trade in Scotland. He was never seen in Norfolk again.

The annual meeting of the Society of Universal Goodwill which took place on 30th November 1787 was said to be the most splendid ever. The Earl of Rosebery made a donation of £20. Sir William Jerningham of Costessey Hall subscribed twenty guineas, in addition to his annual subscription of five guineas. According to the report in this, their tenth year of effective functioning, 'the company dined, and spent the afternoon and evening together with the utmost cheerfulness.' And despite their recent encounter with the rascally Major they all 'seemed to be animated with the genuine spirit of universal goodwill.'

The Workhouse Scandal

In October 1805 Norwich, along with the rest of the country, was celebrating the victorious outcome of the Battle of Trafalgar. At the same time the city was engaged in another battle closer to home, one being waged in the pages of the prestigious *Gentleman's Magazine*. The 'action' had started in late August when a well-known philanthropist by the name of Nield arrived in Norwich. Mr. Nield had been High Sheriff for Buckinghamshire in 1804, but he was better known in his rôle of Philanthropic Treasurer to the Society for Relieving Persons Imprisoned for Small Debts. He had founded this society in 1772 and since that date he had, at his own expense, made three tours of inspection of prisons, places of confinement, and hospitals throughout England. The findings of his 1805 tour were being printed regularly in the *Gentleman's Magazine* with a commentary by a Dr. Lettson.

According to the *Bury and Norwich Post* of 25th August Mr. Nield was favourably impressed by what he saw in the Norfolk and Norwich Hospital. He said the establishment did honour to the county and was one of the best he had visited. 'The wards are lofty,' he wrote, 'and are kept as clean as bedrooms in any private house, being frequently washed and very airy.'

No doubt Dr. Rigby, the Mayor, was pleased. Dr.

Rigby, then in his late fifties, was a man of no small fame himself. As well as being the author of some very important medical books, and a highly-skilled surgeon, he had a literary bent, and was also active in local politics. He was a fervent advocate of vaccination, and in 1788 he had been made a Freeman of the city in recognition of his having ironed out the problems involved in the feeding of the paupers in the local workhouses.

When Mr. Nield, anticipating trouble from petty officials, called on the Mayor to ask permission to visit the main workhouse, Dr. Rigby agreed to take him there himself. Nield recorded his appreciation in his article. 'The worthy Chief Magistrate readily and politely accompanied me,' he wrote. The courteous preliminaries over, the tone of Nield's article changed. From the outset the visitor obviously did not like what he saw. At this date the city workhouse on the bank of the Wensum was known as The Duke's Palace Workhouse, for the good reason that its six hundred-or-so paupers were housed in what had once been the domestic wing of the Duke of Norfolk's Palace. The palace, most of which had been demolished in 1711, had stood on the east side of Duke Street, the mansion and grounds covering a sizeable area between St. Andrew's Street and the river.

The first room into which Nield was taken contained ten single 'cribs', and forty-two beds, and accommodated seventy-four inmates. At its entrance was what Nield described as 'a most offensive and indecent privy, something like a watchman's box'. It was so situated, and so out of repair that privacy was impossible. Worse, it had to be used by both sexes.

This room was not just an unhygienic and overcrowded dormitory. That would have been bad enough in Mr. Nield's eyes. This room was also the paupers' dining-cum-living room. They had to eat and drink sitting on their beds.

Understandably, perhaps, the floor was very dirty, but so were the small casement windows which were almost covered with cobwebs. A leaden sink in the room was used for the disposal of 'every species of filth' while, outside, a stone-sink and water-pipe which might have been used, were out of commission and full of dry rubbish.

According to Nield, the conditions in the other rooms he visited were equally appalling. In one, a family of seven were said to be sharing a single bed. The state of the Boys' Room was insanitary in the extreme. And in Nield's compassionate eyes the appearance of all the paupers was 'singularly squalid, dirty, and miserable, and their clothing ragged and wretched'.

Unbelievably, in view of the fact that Dr. Rigby held the office of Mayor, there was no sick-room or infirmary in the Workhouse. Nield noted with horror that during a small-pox epidemic in July, infected children had been placed with the uninfected in seven different wards, thus increasing the epidemic by around twenty-nine cases, eight of whom had needlessly died.

While Mr. Nield was viewing the rooms, all the paupers except the very old and the infirm, had been herded into the courtyard. Looking out at them Nield was horrified to see a young boy wearing a kind of iron 'yoke' with a central collar that was so padlocked as to make its removal impossible. Complementary to the yoke was an iron ankle-band with a chain, at the end of which was fastened a log of wood. This latter device weighed, all together, no less than twenty-two pounds and the boy had to sleep with both it and the yoke attached to him. He had suffered this already for three weeks, and had still five months and one week of his 'sentence' to serve. The log and chain were removed at certain periods during the day to allow the boy to use his leg in spinning, but they were replaced immediately he had finished his work. On Sundays, as an additional punishment, he spent the day in solitary confinement. All this information Nield had elicited from the boy himself in front of the Mistress of the workhouse who denied nothing. Examining the lad for injuries, Nield found a slight galling on the neck and some scabs and slight 'excoriation' on the ankle. He was told that 'He was twelve years of age; his name was William Rayner; his father dead, and his mother run away.'

Nield requested the Mayor to 'have the goodness to order the irons to be taken off, and that he would oblige me with permission to take them to his house, that the drawing I now inclose might be taken of them.' Nield's restraint snapped as he told Dr. Rigby, 'for these very many years I have not seen the most atrocious felon ironed in so severe a manner'.

What Dr. Rigby replied we do not know. It was someone less wise than him, surely, who told Nield that William Rayner was an incorrigible thief who had many times been imprisoned in the Bridewell. Whoever it was did not know Mr. Nield. The very next morning he was knocking on the door of the Bridewell asking to see the Admissions Book. What he found, after he and the Keeper had searched through the records for ten years past, was that William Rayner had spent two days in the Bridewall, on 18th and 19th April 1804. His crime? Running away from the workhouse! The Keeper swore that he had never been in the prison either before or after those dates. As to his being incorrigible . . . would an 'incorrigible' boy have come running after Nield and the Mayor to thank them so feelingly for his release? Mr. Nield at least did not think so.

Nield concluded his article with some damning figures. The average rate of mortality in the Duke's Palace Workhouse over the last three years had been one in five, unacceptably high. This was only to be expected, he inferred, when people were crowded together in airless rooms and surrounded by filth.

This article appeared in print on 5th September but two days before that, according to the *Bury and Norwich Post*, Dr. Rigby had been taking steps to remedy the deficiencies Nield had uncovered: 'At a well-attended meeting of the Court of Guardians . . . the worthy Mayor urged a material alteration in the medical treatment of the sick in the Workhouse, and [to] abolish the practice of mixing the sick and the healthy'. The Mayor had recommended 'the provision of separate, spacious, clean, and well-ventilated rooms for the reception of persons with infectious diseases'.

It was too late though to save the city's face. On 5th September 1805 Norwich stood indicted in the eyes of the rest of the country as an irresponsible and heartless custodian of the poor. That Nield's article had stirred up dissension even 'within the family' can be inferred from a laudatory paragraph about him in the *Bury and Norwich Post* of 23rd October: 'Who can doubt the veracity of such a disinterested character?' the Editor asks. William Firth could, for one. And his intention was to convince the readership of the *Gentleman's Magazine* that Nield was almost as much of an incorrigible rogue as William Rayner. His letter to that end was written on 16th November.

William Firth was a highly-respected manufacturer in the city, a Steward of Norwich, and in 1805 a Guardian of the Poor. His letter to the magazine started, 'It was with a mingled emotion of indignation and contempt that I read . . . a communication of a Mr. Nield respecting the Old Workhouse in this city, and the punishment of William Rayner, an incorrigible boy . . .' He then continued for several paragraphs to denigrate Mr. Nield and his activities in near-libellous terms. Basking in the after-glow of Trafalgar, he obviously thought attack the best means of defence. His main bone of contention was that Nield had been well aware that the Duke's Palace Workhouse was about to be closed, and that a new workhouse, which Nield had seen

The Duke's Palace in the 18th century. The Dukes of
Norfolk had a succession of town houses on this site from
the 16th century. The last was built c. 1672 and mostly
demolished in 1711. The remnant became one of the
city's workhouses.

and approved, was almost completed. That he had not thought fit to disclose this in his article showed how devious he was. Nield's observations on the treatment of smallpox cases Firth managed to construe as a sinister attack on inoculation. He mocked Nield's concern about the punishment of the boy, Rayner, informing him jocularly that the iron 'yoke' was known to its familiars as 'the pot-hooks'. He told a highly unlikely tale of how it was Rayner's 'sport and delight' to draw little boys about the court-yard on the log! And he finished this spirited case for the defence by the most ludicrous 'non-sequitur' of all. He accused Mr. Nield of hiding himself in the gaoler's bed-chamber in the County Gaol on the approach of a visiting magistrate, thus throwing doubt on 'his intent being so pure and charitable as the visiting the abodes of wretchedness would naturally infer.'

It was left to poor John Gurney of Earlham, father of Elizabeth Fry, to wipe the egg from the city's collective face. He did his best in a dignified letter published in the *Gentleman's Magazine* in December. He answered Nield's criticisms point by point, sometimes admitting the justice of them, more often claiming they were inaccurate. For example he refused to admit that a room measuring seventy-four foot by thirty would be 'overcrowded' by seventy-four inmates. He explained that the 'privy' so abhorred by Nield was actually a 'night-stool' and only used by the elderly who could not go downstairs. The story of a family of seven sharing a bed was not true, he said. One child slept in the Girls' Room. And two shared a crib by their mother's bed. He detailed the cleaning arrangements in the workhouse and showed that they were adequate. 'As to the case of the boy Rayner . . .' Here Gurney very subtly conceded a point. The 'incorrigible lad' needed 'a strong and striking measure of coercion.' The mode of punishment used was not 'severe in effect'. Nevertheless, he had to agree it did look rather unpleasant. And since it might be misused by less humane Guardians, he considered it might be wise to ban its use in the future.

On the whole John Gurney sounded hurt rather than angered by what Mr. Nield had done to Norwich. He pointed out that the philanthropist knew that the old work-house was about to be vacated. When the Master was preparing for the transfer of six hundred souls from one building to another, was it any wonder that there was some lack of order? Why had Mr. Nield not made allowances?

Needless to say, Mr. Gurney was told why in a reply that was printed in the *Gentleman's Magazine* in January 1806. Nield and Dr. Lettson stuck to their guns. Nield knew what he had seen and what he had been told. Doubtless he was used to this sort of reaction both in public and in private. And his visit to Norwich had accomplished much. The magistrates could now assemble in the parlour of the gaol without danger of suffocation, the sewer having been re-paired. There was an isolation-ward in the new workhouse. And the degrading punishment suffered by twelve-year-old William Rayner would never again be inflicted upon a pauper, no matter how 'incorrigible'.

John Crome

John Crome was born in December 1768 in the parish of
St. George, Tombland, in which church his baptism was
registered. It is known that his father was a journeyman-
weaver and an alehouse-keeper, a common combination of
trades in Norwich until well into the 19th Century. Some
authorities state categorically that Crome, the elder, was
landlord of an inn called The Griffin, which stood where the
Anglia Television building now stands on the corner of
King Street and Prince of Wales Road. Others say more
cautiously that Crome was born 'in the Castle Ditches'. On
the other hand, a recently-published architectural map of
the city locates the artist's birthplace as being a 17th century
building on St. Martin-at-Palace Plain. That there should be
such contradictory statements emphasizes how humble
were Crome's origins, compared to the well-documented
beginnings of John Constable, born eight years later of an
affluent, middle-class Suffolk family. It also underlines the
fact that Crome left very few written records about his life,
and certainly nothing in the nature of a memoir. The few
public records that document his progress through a span of
fifty-three years are fleshed out by oral history, namely
anecdotes told of him, and by him, and handed down
through the generations.

We know something of the Norwich into which Crome

was born. It was a busy, prosperous city whose main industry was worsted-weaving, but where trades such as leather-working and brewing also thrived. It was an important port and market-centre, and had a sufficient number of wealthy residents to give it the 'genteel' air, so prized in that era. How much the city valued this gentility is seen in the advertisements which appeared in the local newspapers in the 1760s. In the *Norwich Mercury* of 15th March 1766 it was reported that, 'On Monday morning early the scaffold before Ivory's Building in Surrey Street was taken down. The Houses make a most noble appearance and are finished in such Taste as does honour to the Architect. Of the present buildings only one is at this time occupied owing to the Proprietors not being able to finish it till next Michaelmas. The Projector, we hear, when his plan is completed, will have ten more elegant Houses with every necessary Conveniency for genteel private families, as Coach House, and Stables, etc. To each Dwelling, with Proper Offices. At the entrance to the Court Yard will be, on each side of the Great Gates, a Porter's Lodge. The whole, when executed, will greatly contribute to the elegance of this part of the City. As such Dwellings are greatly wanted in this flourishing and populous place, we make no doubt but the Proprietor will . . . meet with due encouragement.'

By the time John Crome was born there were buildings all over Norwich to testify to Thomas Ivory's genius, the principal ones being the Methodist Meeting-House in Bishopgate, the Octagon Chapel in Colegate, the Assembly House, and the Theatre.

Not every resident of Norwich basked in the sunshine of prosperity. In September 1766 when Mr. Ivory's Surrey Street building was completed, there was a full-scale riot in the city due to 'the great scarcity and the price of provisions'. The poor and desperate attacked the New Mills, ransacked houses in the city, then marched to Trowse where they committed similar depredations. The following year two of the ringleaders were hanged on Castle Hill.

It was between these two societies – the prosperous and the wretchedly impoverished – that families like the Cromes had to steer an often precarious course. Working-life had to start early. We do not know what schooling, if any, John Crome had. From what he told his friends, he was sent to stand at the age of thirteen, on the Maddermarket where youngsters were hired as domestic servants and unskilled assistants. It was Crome's good fortune to be taken on as errand-boy by Dr. Edward Rigby whose house stood near the junction of St. Giles Street and Bethel Street, opposite the top end of Willow Lane. Rigby was one of a circle of gifted polymaths who were active in Norwich public life in the late 18th and early 19th centuries. He was the grandson of Dr. John Taylor, Presbyterian minister of the Octagon Chapel, and at the age of thirty-four was already a respected surgeon. Later he would gain fame as radical politician, energetic mayor, pioneer of vaccination, dietician, agriculturalist, philosopher, writer, and for fathering quads! Amongst his circle of friends were several wealthy and cultured families who, in future years, were to give John Crome patronage or employment.

Crome worked in the Rigby household for two years. From this period comes the apocryphal story of his having destroyed a skeleton, which Rigby's students had laid in the boy's bed, by hurling it out of a garret window. This was a good 'pub-tale' which Crome apparently enjoyed relating and is probably true. Obviously not fitted to be a surgeon's apprentice, but in need of a trade, the young Crome, and his family no doubt, looked elsewhere. Not far from Dr Rigby's house, a few doors along from the Coach and Horses pub in Bethel Street, was the shop of Francis Whisler, house and coach painter. (This building was destroyed in an air-raid in 1942). Here, in

August 1783, John Crome began his apprenticeship. There were plenty of diversions for young lads in Norwich in the 1780s. In April 1784 John Crome doubtless witnessed the arrival of Sir John Wodehouse, candidate in the County Election, with over two thousand horsemen and a band. They arrived in the city via St. Giles, and the procession wended its way across the market-place where thousands of cheering, or jeering, spectators sported the colours of their favoured men.

Then there were the balloon-ascents, still a novelty, but increasing in frequency. On 1st June 1784 Mr. Decker went up in a balloon from Quantrell's Gardens, (which were located in Queens Road, near the St. Stephen's round-about). To the admiration of the spectators he stayed in the air for almost half-an-hour. The following month Major Money, a well-known Norwich citizen, made a famous flight from the same gardens for the benefit of the Norwich and Norfolk Hospital. Blown off course and out to sea he was miraculously rescued at half-past-eleven that night by a revenue-cutter off Lowestoft.

It was during his apprenticeship years that Crome became friendly with Robert Ladbrooke, another aspiring young artist who was apprenticed to Mr. White, printer and engraver, of London Lane. It is said that the pair got together and made a tentative start in the realm of commercial art, Crome producing landscapes and Ladbrooke portraits. Different as they were in temperament, Crome and Ladbrooke were to have a close relationship, until a public quarrel divided them in 1816. Their future wives were sisters, and many of the stories about Crome's youth have come down to us in the memoirs of Henry Ladbrooke, Robert's son.

On 2nd October 1792 John Crome married Phoebe Berney in the church of St. Mary's, Coslany. Four weeks later his baby daughter was born. Like many working-class lads for whom marriage had become a necessity, the event had to be delayed for as long as possible because of lack of money. At twenty-three Crome had a wife, a baby, and a modest home, north of the river in Colegate. He was still doing work as a journeyman for Mr. Whisler. At the same age John Constable would begin *his* studies at the Royal Academy School in London, supported by an allowance from his father.

Already there is evidence in the events of Crome's life that someone had spotted his talent. He got the job of drawing-master to a son of William Sparshall, the Quaker wine-merchant who lived beside St. Clement's Church. More important, he was befriended by Mr. Thomas Harvey of Catton, a wealthy member of a notable Norwich family, who had his own private gallery of masterpieces, and who entertained noted and established artists such as the portrait-painter, Sir William Beechey. Mr. Harvey's house must surely have been to Crome the equivalent of the Royal Academy School. While earning a living he worked on his landscapes; he painted the Cow Tower, Norwich from Hellesdon Gravel Pits, and scenes on the river. Meanwhile his family, now living in a comfortable house in Gildengate (today's St. George's Street) was growing. In 1794 his first son, John Berney, was born. In 1796 another boy, Frederick James, arrived. It must have been a relief to Crome when he obtained the post of drawing-master to the wealthy and influential Gurney family of Earlham.

A sad notice had appeared in the *Bury and Norwich Post* of 21st November 1792: 'Died on Sunday last, at Earlham Hall, in the 38th year of her age, Mrs. Catherine Gurney . . . the mother of eleven children'. We know from an entry in the journal of sixteen-year-old Richenda Gurney, that by January 1798 'Crome' (as she referred to him) was established there. His Gurney pupils at this time, in addition to Richenda, were eighteen-year-old Betsey, who was to

John Crome. A portrait by Hannah Gurney, 1786–1850.

become Mrs. Elizabeth Fry two years later, and Hannah, Louisa, and Priscilla who were fifteen, fourteen, and thirteen respectively. The relationship between master and pupils seems to have been a very happy one and in 1802 and 1806 Crome accompanied the family on their annual holiday to the Lake District.

It was at Earlham that Crome met Amelia and John Opie, two of the brightest stars in the local artistic firmament. Amelia, a renowned local beauty, was a novelist and diarist. John Opie was a portrait painter of no mean reputation. Crome was eventually on such friendly terms with Opie that, according to Amelia, they sometimes worked jointly on a canvas and her husband painted the sky in Crome's picture of Carrow Abbey.

In 1803 an event took place which was significant both for Norwich and for John Crome. This was the formation of the Norwich Society whose aim was avowedly to instigate, 'An Enquiry into the Rise, Progress, and Present State of Painting, Architecture, and Sculpture, with a view to point out the Best Methods of Study to attain Greater Perfection in the Arts'. The moving spirits behind the Society were initially Dr. Edward Rigby, R. Mackenzie Bacon, (Editor of the *Norwich Mercury*), Dr. Frank Sayers, (physician and polymath) and Dr. Forster, (Master of the Grammar School). What they had done was prepare the ground for the Norwich School of Painters which was to survive through three generations of local artists and of which John Crome is regarded as the founder.

By 1803 Phoebe Crome had borne six children, three of whom had died. She was pregnant again in the summer of 1804 when John and Robert Ladbrooke went off to Wales on a sketching holiday. One wonders whether she ever complained either about John's holidays, or about his evening visits to his favourite pubs. The Rifleman tavern in Cross Lane (now the Little Portion Mission House), the

Black Bull in Magdalen Street, and the Three Cranes in the Lower Close all apparently did well by Crome's custom. The Norwich Society too had initially met in a pub, the Hole-In-The-Wall Tavern off Exchange Street. Then in 1805 it moved to Sir Benjamin Wrench's Court at the junction of Little Cockey Lane and Pottergate where they held their first exhibition, twenty-two of the pictures coming from John Crome.

Looking at his tranquil scenes on the Wensum and the Yare we might forget that there was another barbaric face to Crome's Norwich. In July 1803 according to a report in the *Bury and Norwich Post* a petty criminal was knocked unconscious by missiles thrown by the mob while he was in the pillory on Castle Hill. He was taken away, examined by doctors, then 'deemed in a state to be replaced in the pillory'. On 6th April 1805 on the same day that a man was publicly hanged 'on the New Drop' on Castle Hill, another was whipped in the market-place.

As an artist Crome was now going from strength to strength. In 1806 he exhibited his first two paintings at the Royal Academy then in 1807 and 1808 he became President of the Norwich Society. From this period came works like *Slate Quarries* originating, it is thought, in his Welsh sojourn with Ladbrooke, and *Moonlight on the Yare*, which hangs in the Tate Gallery. In other pictures from this period his living trees quiver in their summer foliage, one *Woodland Scene* depicting part of Chapel Field Gardens.

In 1811 John Crome was in his forty-third year but already he was 'Old Crome' by virtue of the fact that his eldest son, John Berney Crome, was exhibiting too. Indeed in this year John Berney, at seventeen years, had his first picture exhibited in the Academy. John Crome had been thirty-eight before he had attained that distinction. But then John Berney did not have his father's responsibilities. By 1811 John had six children, the youngest only a year old.

For most of his married life precious hours had been used up in teaching, in travelling to the homes of pupils, or in attending auction-sales in his rôle as art-dealer. The wonder is that by the end of his fifty-three years he had exhibited 307 paintings.

In 1814 when Crome's seventh and last child, Michael, was a year old, this very 'local' painter made his first and last foreign excursion. It was a trip to Paris to see Napoleon's booty of plundered works of art which were on show in the Tuileries. For an artist of Crome's talent and limited opportunities such a trip was not a luxury. Yet in one of his very few surviving letters to his wife we detect a sense almost of guilt as he promises her that he will make the journey pay and will be very careful how he lays out his money. In the end we all reaped the benefit of Crome's excursion in three marvellous pictures. *Bruges River/ Moonlight*, and *View in Paris – Italian Boulevard* were painted in 1814–15. *The Fishmarket at Boulogne* was painted c. 1820 from a sketch made by Crome in 1814. All three can be seen in Norwich Castle Museum.

Crome was now drawing-master at Norwich Grammar School where his son John Berney was Head Boy in 1813. Robert Ladbrooke was also a well-known and respected art-teacher. Ladbrooke was reputedly sober, industrious and thrifty. Crome was easy-going, egregious and endearingly mischievious at times. It was this clash of personalities which led to the quarrel between the two in 1816. Ladbrooke thought that the surplus funds of the Norwich Society should be utilised in buying materials to help local artists. Crome was determined they should be used for conviviality, as had always been the case. In the end Robert Ladbrooke left the Society and with some other well-known local artists founded a splinter-group which exhibited for two years in a building on the site of today's Central Library.

There ought to have been years of work ahead of John Crome. In those magnificent large canvases *Mousehold Heath, Norwich* and *Poringland Oak* which both hang in the Tate we see an artist in his prime. Whether he suffered from some undocumented chronic illness we do not know but in April 1821 while working on the preliminary sketch for the *Yarmouth Water Frolic* he was stricken by what was described as 'a fever'. He died within two weeks, but not before there had been a moving reconciliation with Robert Ladbrooke.

There is a memorial to Crome in the church of St. George, Colegate where he was buried in the south aisle chapel, but his true memorials hang today all over the world, in galleries and private collections, giving pleasure to millions. No small achievement for the Norwich working-lad who stood on the Maddermarket one autumn day in 1781 waiting to see what life had in store for him.

John Bilby

The manuscript journal of John Bilby is a fascinating account of the life-pattern of an ordinary young man, a barber, who lived in Norwich at the beginning of the 19th century.

John Bilby was something of an extrovert, a decidedly convivial character who took a lively interest in the passing scene. We see this not so much in the journal itself, but in his account of a coach journey tacked on at the end. John made the journey with his mother in 1828. They set out from The White Swan in Norwich one June morning as St. Peter's clock struck six, John seated on the Box beside the coachman, Mr. Marshall. By the time they left Dereham at eight o'clock, he and Mr. Marshall were sharing a bottle of gin. On the second day of the journey, between Peterborough and Lincoln, John and a sea-captain became boon companions. 'This man soon pleased me with his manner of causing mirth,' he tells us. At Nottingham the coach dropped them at The Black's Head Inn. 'Too grand,' was John's verdict. He asked the coachman to find them a more homely place. He did, and the food was uneatable. The landlord was a 'deep-looking old fellow; a wig to cover his upper works, rather sullen, and spoke in a slow voice and short sentences'.

To raise their spirits Bilby took his mother for a walk in the park. An old man invited them into his cottage. There were two turtle doves hanging at the door in a cage and seven cows in the yard. They had rum and new milk. As always with John Bilby the day had turned out well after all.

John Bilby, barber, citizen of Norwich had been born in Yarmouth in 1801. He had been only a year old, when his family moved to Norwich. They had lived first in Ber Street then in King Street where, he tells us, he was first 'put to playschool at Mrs. Bunting's'. After a few years the family moved to St. Augustine's then, shortly afterwards, to a more convenient rented house in St. Saviour's, near Stump Cross. This remained the family home until John married, and possibly after that.

Four days after John's seventh birthday, his father died. There were three other children, Thomas, Charlotte, and Peter. Thomas must have been several years John's elder for in 1809 he enlisted as a soldier in the Twelfth Regiment of Foot. Wellington had begun his Peninsular Campaign the previous year, so cannon-fodder was in demand. It was to be eight years before this brother returned to Norwich, probably wounded, since he had been awarded a pension of 9d a day for life.

In 1811 John's mother re-married and shortly after he was found a position as errand-boy in the home of Mr. Willemont, a master-weaver. He was ten years old. When he was eleven he went to live and work with Mr. Horth of London Street, an appraiser. From Mr. Horth's he moved to Mr. Leeds, a brushmaker, in St. Andrew's parish. He lived here for two years but his job came to an end when Mr. Leeds went bankrupt. He then went to a tailor called Mr. Ling where he remained until it was time for him to start an apprenticeship. On 20th August 1815 he was signed as an apprentice to Mr. Mason, tailor and hairdresser, of King Street. He was not yet fourteen years old.

After two years with Mr. Mason, John and he had a disagreement. John went to another haircutter and dresser to finish his training. In 1818 his sister, Charlotte, married. John omits to tell us the date of his own marriage but relates how he met his future wife on the Nelson Steam Packet going to Yarmouth on a pleasure-trip. It sounds very much in character.

John apparently had talents appropriate to his trade. For he was an important member of *The Musical Sons of Good Humours*, a vocal and instrumental society. He was awarded a star-medal for serving as secretary to it. In 1822 came the supreme accolade. He was elected President. It was also the year when he was 'engaged by the Norwich Company of Comedians to take the part of a Knight of the Garter in the play of the Coronation of George IV, [and] appeared on the stage for 16 nights'. This production was well written-up in local papers.

On 21st January the *Norfolk Chronicle* contained the following advertisement: 'In consequence of extensive preparations, the opening of the Theatre is necessarily postponed until Thursday 31st January when will be represented *The CORONATION of HIS Majesty George IV*. As performed at the Theatre Royal, Drury Lane. The Dresses and Regalia and every other Decoration are copied from the models of the Theatre Royal, Drury Lane, By Permission of the Proprietor. The Whole of the Company with Numerous Additional Aid both Vocal and Instrumental will be employed to give every possible effect to this splendid ceremony. After which will be performed the *Comedy of A Cure For The Heart Ache.*'

There was a review of the production in the *Bury and Norwich Post* of 6th February: 'The Theatre opened on Thursday night with the grand spectacle of *The Coronation*, as represented at Drury Lane. It seems that Mr. Elliston has allowed a Mr. Lee, who was connected with the preparation of the pageant at that house, to make a reduced copy. And he transports his scenes, decorations, and properties, together with the Champion and his horse and armour, to gratify the provinces. The expense is stated to be unprecedented. Nearly 200 persons were upon the scene during the banquet. The Champion and his little charger deserved unqualified praise . . . The Coronation anthem was respectably chorused, and the music supported by an organ. His Majesty is resplendent in gold. . . .'

The critic from the *Norfolk Chronicle* was a little more condescending; 'a copy of a copy, the Pageant, very effectively got up, went off with all the éclat that could be expected from its exhibition on a stage of such narrow dimensions . . . the only reform which we would petition for applies to the appointment of organist. The Royal Banquet in Westminster Hall is extremely well arranged. The Equestrian Champion's entry and challenge the most exciting part of the whole proceedings.'

While this noble fare was on the menu at the Theatre Royal, there were less elevated entertainments on offer elsewhere. There were sparring-matches at pubs. Wombwell's Menagerie was on Castle Hill. There was 'Cocking' at the White Swan Inn behind St. Peter Mancroft's, the Gentlemen of Norwich against the Gentlemen of Northampton. Also at the White Swan was a curious exhibition called *The Papyreum*. This consisted of 130 figures fashioned out of folded paper, 'figures of various nations, their peculiar expressions of countenance, customs, and costume, architecture, landscape, and flowers'. Each week in the local newspapers another titillating detail was added. The models had been made 'from a bed of sickness from which the interesting artist was not able to move for the last four years of her life'. The 'artist' it was later revealed, was a 'Mrs. Aberdein'. No doubt this was all designed to bring in the customers. With an admission charge of one-and-sixpence, a shilling for working-people and children, some persuasion was probably required.

The Theatre Royal in 1805, a contemporary illustration
published by T. Woodfall. The first Norwich Theatre,
designed by Thomas Ivory, opened in 1758. It was
extensively remodelled by William Wilkins, senior, in
1801.

Life in Bilby's Norwich was not all plays and pleasure. There was plenty of strife and a simmering unrest constantly under the surface. This would erupt in frightening outbreaks of violence such as happened on 5th March 1822 when six men who had destroyed threshing-machines in the Attleborough/Buckenham area were brought to the city to be imprisoned. They were escorted by a detachment of Eye Yeomanry Cavalry. As soon as the soldiers were spied at St. Stephen's Gates a mob gathered and began to stone them. The soldiers threatened to open fire but the crowd stood their ground. When the Yeomanry went into an inn all its windows were broken. The rioters dispersed only when the Mayor arrived with the City police.

While this was happening in St. Stephen's another disturbance had broken out at the Castle Ditches. One of the Buckenham prisoners had just been brought in by a constable and the crowd outside the gaol were after the constable's skin. Two warders were sent out with him as a bodyguard but as soon as they entered Golden Ball Lane they were attacked. Their cart was seized and thrown in the river. The constable and his horse narrowly escaped the same fate. According to the *Bury and Norwich Post* the trouble was caused by 'the loose and disorderly boys who frequent our streets. The industrious classes take no part'.

What John Bilby thought of all this we shall never know. His journal entries were of happier events: '25th March 1822 – First Feast Day of the Sons of Good Humours.' 31st December 1822: 'A good frolic with egg-flip to finish the old year out and welcome the New Year in.'

John Bilby was of 'the industrious classes'. He had had an outstandingly successful year. He was just twenty-one-years old.

The Troubled Textile Trade

R. H. Mottram once described the Yarn Factory near Whitefriars Bridge (now part of Jarrold's Printing Works) as representing 'the last effort to uphold the Norwich woollen trade against the encroaching and finally victorious competition of the powerlooms of the North of England'. This building might also be regarded as a kind of war memorial, a reminder of the long years of bitter struggle and strife which preceded the demise of the Norwich cloth industry.

Industrialization did play a major part in the decline of Norwich's cloth industry but it was not solely to blame. Berry's *Norwich Directory* (1811) stated: 'At present the merchants being shut out of foreign markets by war, and from our own by fashion, the number of hands employed must be considerably reduced. The principal articles of this manufactory are bombazines and broad camlets, for the latter of which the East India Company have annually given large orders.'

A variety of factors brought about a situation where for generations the city's cloth workers led a precarious seesawing existence, periods of comparative prosperity alternating with ones of severe financial hardship. As E. P. Thompson has pointed out,[1] it was wage-cutting more than anything else that gradually undermined the status of the handloom-

[1] *The Making Of The English Working Classes*

weaver, and it was against wage-cutting that the most bitter battles were fought in Norwich, some of them engendering the kind of riotous behaviour that occurred in July 1822.

According to a report in the *Norfolk Chronicle* of 13th July 1822 the trouble began on Friday 5th July. There was a meeting of the city's principal cloth manufacturers in the Guildhall. One of these manufacturers had written to the *Chronicle* in March warning that the manufacture of bomba-zines and crepes was suffering badly from articles being made in the North at a much lower rate of wages, and advising immediate wage-cutting in Norwich. His fellow manufacturers were now following his advice. On 5th July it was resolved to reduce rates of pay to the weavers by 1½d to 2d per dozen pieces. The following morning the new rates were announced to the journeymen weavers with predictable results.

On the morning of Sunday 7th July there was a meeting of around 150 weavers in Friary Yard close to St. James's Church in Cowgate (now 'Whitefriars'). Two weavers were appointed from each parish to summon those neigh-bours who were both weavers and householders to another meeting the following day. At this second meeting about 1,100 weavers attended. They drew up a petition and marched with it in a body to the home of Alderman J. W. Robberds who was Deputy Chairman of the Manufac-turers' Committee. The Chairman, John Harvey, Esq., was travelling on the continent. Robberds lived in Grout's Court off Magdalen Street and had a camlet factory in St. Saviour's Lane. He was no friend of the weavers but on this occasion he complied with their request that the manufac-turers should meet again to reconsider their decision. He called a meeting of his fellow manufacturers for the follow-ing day, Tuesday 9th July in the Guildhall. At a mass-rally on Mousehold Heath that Monday afternoon the weavers decided they ought to have representatives at the manufacturers' meeting. Early on Tuesday morning Alderman Robberds was presented with the proposition that fifty-four weavers should be admitted to the conference. In the end he agreed to admit a dozen.

By the time the meeting was due to start on that July Tuesday a huge crowd had gathered in the market-place. As the manufacturers arrived at the Guildhall each was greeted according to his popularity, or lack of it, with the workers. Mr. Arthur Beloe appears to have been Norwich's counterpart to the renowned Colonel Joseph Hanson, the Manchester manufacturer who championed the cause of local weavers. Before Beloe went into the Guildhall he made a speech stating that he was against wage-cutting and also against such decisions having been taken in the absence of John Harvey, Esq., who did not favour wage-reductions. Beloe promised that he would keep to the old rates no matter what was said about Yorkshire competition. As was to be expected his statements were greeted with vociferous cheering and great applause.

To most of the manufacturers at the conference table wage-cutting was seen as the only way of saving a threatened industry. The weavers replied that if wages were lowered they would not be able to live. Most of them worked in their own homes and since the beginning of the Napoleonic Wars both house rents and the price of coals had risen steeply. Moreover, they declared, to lower wages would lower the quality of the cloth produced and would bring the trade into disrepute.

By four-thirty that afternoon the conference was still in full swing. No doubt the crowd in the market-place was growing restless and excitable as they waited for some public announcement to be made. It was a bad moment for William Bossley, a local manufacturer, to arrive at the Guildhall. The porch of the building was now crowded with people eager to find out what was being said inside.

Tempers snapped as Mr. Bossley tried to push his way through to the conference room. He was shoved violently back down the stairs into the midst of the crowd. At this point the savagery latent in the 'mob' came frighteningly to the surface. Bossley suddenly became the target for communal fear and frustration. He was knocked to the ground, beaten and kicked, his hat, shoes and coat torn off him. Only the efforts of some humane souls in the crowd prevented what would probably have been a horrific murder. They pulled him free of his assailants so that he was able to run into a shop in Cockey Lane (now 'London Street'). While some of the mob broke the shop-windows others threw the torn-up remnants of Bossley's coat and hat triumphantly into the air.

The news of the assault on Mr. Bossley soon reached his colleagues inside the Guildhall. Steps were immediately taken to quell a full-scale riot. Firstly a message was sent to the commanding officer of the 7th Dragoon Guards at the Barracks, asking him to put his men at the ready. Then a placatory announcement was made from the balcony of the Guildhall. The crowd was told that the manufacturers had agreed not to cut wages. This announcement (which was untrue, but understandable in the circumstances) was greeted by applause and the waving of hats. Shortly afterwards a body of Dragoons galloped into the market-place and drew up in formation in front of the north doors of the Guildhall. We are not told the reaction of the crowd, only the fact that the Mayor and the magistrates hastily thanked their officer for bringing his men so promptly but assured him that their presence was not needed.

Was it the withdrawal of the Dragoons or the reappearance of the popular Arthur Beloe that changed the angry mood of the crowd? The latter was obviously a charismatic character. He was loudly cheered and a large body of weavers accompanied him as he made his way to his new factory on Orford Hill. Later, a procession led by a band set off from Beloe's factory to parade through the city streets. Some of the weavers carried placards saying 'God Bless Arthur Beloe', others held up samples of Norwich manufactured goods. Beer was doled out to the appreciative spectators.

Inevitably the weavers lost this battle in the end. So did their champion, Arthur Beloe. On 9th March 1830 his premises, which had been erected at a cost of more than £4000 were sold by auction for £860. Similar battles were to be fought time and time again in Norwich while the cloth industry was in its dying throes. Many of them are detailed in the Report of Dr. James Mitchell, one of the Assistant Commissioners of the Handloom Commission of Inquiry, who arrived in the city in April 1838.

Dr. Mitchell heard how, in 1829, Mr. Henry Willet, a very large manufacturer, and a magistrate, had been attacked by a mob of several hundreds as he walked home from his warehouse in Pottergate Street. Only the inter-vention of the popular Cathedral cleric, Mr. Prebendary Wodehouse, had saved Willet's life. Willet escaped into a courtyard and the clergyman stationed himself in the narrow entry and kept the crowd at bay.

John Wright whose factory was on Elm Hill and who lived in Bishopgate Street had been waylaid just as Willet had been, but with direr consequences. Vitriol had been thrown in his face and he lost the sight of his right eye. When Dr. Mitchell met Wright in 1838 he wore a large green eye-shade. He declined to give evidence, as did many other manufacturers, through fear of the consequences.

Mitchell was told that since 1833 there had been no open rioting by the weavers because they had a strong Weavers' Union Committee to organize their industrial action. The Secretary of this Committee was Samuel Fish who was also landlord of the Turkey Cock pub in Wensum Street. Fish

The Yarn Factory. Completed in 1837, the building
changed its function c. 1906 when it became the home
of Jarrolds Printing Works, and, briefly, of Caley's
Crackers.

fought unflaggingly for his weavers and for the standing of the handloom-weaving trade. His chief adversary among the manufacturers was Mr. John Clarke, of Churton and Clarke, bombazine manufacturers, of St. George's Cole-gate. At the beginning of 1838, Mitchell was told, Clarke began to pay his weavers less than list prices. Samuel Fish and another committee-member visited Clarke and gave him a warning. According to Clarke, the latter replied, '*I* warn *you* to go down stairs!'. Within days Clarke had a strike on his hands, one that lasted for over two months, until the very eve of Assistant Commissioner Mitchell's visit. According to Clarke, his premises were 'watched' night and day by union-men: 'They stopped my hands and advised them to carry back their work. Whenever I went out, they sent someone to follow me'.

The union was also determined to stop manufacturers like Clarke sending out work to the country handloom-weavers who would work for less than the agreed wage. On 21st March 1838 there was a report in the *Norfolk Chronicle* of a weaver named Allen being arrested five miles out of the city for annoying a carrier 'who had been up to Mr. Clarke's in Calvert Street'.

On 7th March the *Chronicle* had reported another court case in which Mr. Clarke had been the defendant, 'sum-moned before the Magistrates on the information of Mr. Samuel Fish . . . charged with having paid a weaver named James Harris 6s 6d in coals, in part of his wages'. An Act had been passed against 'Truck', or payment in goods, so this was an offence. Mr. Clarke was exonerated by his fellow-magistrates and Samuel Fish had to pay all costs.

One of the reasons frequently cited for the unhealthy state of the Norwich cloth industry was the weavers' hostility to the power-loom. The local 'authority' on the use of machinery in the textile-trade was Mr. Dodshen Blake, manager of the yarn-factory, who gave evidence to Mr.

Mitchell. Blake gave it as his opinion that it was 'to machinery the city must in future look for its prosperity'. It was this point of view, shared by a group of wealthy businessmen in the city, that had led to the formation of the Norwich Yarn Company in September 1833. Out of a population of about 61,500 there were 7,000 receiving poor-relief. The poor-rate was unacceptably high. Norwich imported yarn for its looms from the industrial North. The idea of spinning yarn by power in Norwich itself seemed to make good sense. On 11th September 1833 shares in the Yarn Company were advertised in the *Bury and Norwich Post* the aim of the company being stated as 'to form an Establishment for the Spinning of Worstead Yarn by Machinery . . . a source of great employment to our intelligent artisans and their industrious families.'

The shares were bought up so rapidly that the city's poor-law Guardians, who had initially purchased an interest in the company, were able to withdraw their shares by mid-October. By the last week of October the site of the first worsted mill, on a former orchard beside St. Edmund's church was being cleared, and a fifty-horse engine had been ordered for it. At the end of February 1834 the ceremony of laying the foundation stone took place. Workers from the small Lakenham Yarn Mill, then under Mr. Blake's management, made up a 'Bishop Blaise' procession, a historic piece of pageantry in honour of the patron-saint of wool-combers. They walked from Lakenham to the site of the new factory in St. Edmund's, woolcombers, sorters, spinners, drawers, twisters, transformed into shepherds and shepherdesses, Jason and his Argonauts, Bishop Blaise and his attendants. It was a grand public relations exercise designed to counteract the negative industrial action of rebellious weavers. Mayor Samuel Bignold, the founding father of the Yarn Company spread the mortar with a silver trowel. The building, which was burned down in 1913, was

160 feet long, forty-two foot broad, four storeys high, and capable of accommodating 5,000 spindles.

By July 1835 the St. Edmund's Factory was thriving. The Directors stated that half-a-dozen such factories would hardly meet the current demand for Norwich-spun yarn. That year they secured the Holkham clip and they spun this as a separate parcel of yarn because of the particularly high reputation of the Holkham fleece.

The Yarn Company was still doing well in April 1836 so it was decided to build a second factory. They bought the premises of Mr. Youngman, a dyer, on the east side of Cowgate Street, between Whitefriars Bridge and Friary Yard. The first stone of this new factory, the St. James's Factory was laid on 1st December 1836. Again there was a Bishop Blaise procession, a much larger one than in 1834. Again Mr. Samuel Bignold laid the foundation stone, assisted by Mr. Parkinson, the architect, and Messrs Wilson, Cattermoul and Darkins, the contractors. Mr. Bignold said the building was to be 163 feet by 42, four storeys high, and would be worked by two 80-horse power steam-engines. It would employ 1200 people as compared with the 800 employed in the St. Edmund's factory.

Work on the St. James's factory building proceeded much more slowly than its predecessor, possibly because the Company ran out of funds. On 21st June 1837 a report in the *Bury and Norwich Post* spoke of the foundation of the new factory being nearly completed and calling upon the public 'for further subscription to complete this building in which it is intended to introduce a species of manufacture which would contribute to an increased business both in spinning and weaving'. It was not until 10th November that the newspaper could report the completion of the new 165-foot-tall chimney of the new Yarn Factory near Whitefriars Bridge. At the 'topping-out' ceremony a band on top of the building played national airs and 'God Save the Queen', a flag was hoisted and guns were fired.

In White's *Directory* for 1845 'the large worsted mill in St. Edmund's where yarn of the finest quality is now spun' was said to employ upwards of 300 hands. The larger factory in St. James's was let off in rooms to various manufacturers 'who have here about 600 power looms.' The report of a disturbance at the St. James's Factory in January 1850 indicates that the greater part of the work-force was by then female. When a silk-winder called Douglas tried to change the working-hours there was a near-riot: 'The females became much excited, and finding out who had been behind the change, pelted Mr. Douglas with snowballs and mud as he was going home on Friday evening, and threatened to throw him in the river. They also broke several windows of the factory and of his house. The next day the 700 employees left off work, saying they could not stand for five hours without a break, and that this prevented them attending to their families. On Monday they stayed out again and the manufacturers agreed to return to the old hours'.

That same year the Yarn Company went bankrupt. No-one could fail to hear the death-knell of the city's textile trade. Already shoe-factories, breweries, and iron-foundries were giving its citizens a living. Eventually St. James's factory no longer resounded to the whirring of spindles and the clatter of looms, but fortunately it remained a building with a purpose. Because of this it has survived as an impressive memorial to Norwich's renowned cloth-industry, and to all those who worked and fought for it.

Father Ignatius

Joseph Lyne moved into the house on Elm Hill with ten companions in January 1864. He was twenty-seven years old and a man of dreams and visions. The house was to be 'The Priory of St. Mary and St. Dunstan' and he, Joseph Lyne, became 'Father Ignatius'. Francis Kilvert, clergyman and diarist, met Joseph in Wales in 1870. He was much struck by the unusual beauty of his fine forehead and his soft, dark eyes which would suddenly blaze with a strange wildness when he was moved. He seems to have possessed that quality which is called 'charisma' but, unhappily, that was no protection against the bigotry and ignorance of Victorian Norwich.

The Priory Chapel was opened at the end of February. There was a description of both building and ceremony in the *Bury and Norwich Post*. The Monastery was in an old court on Elm Hill near St. Andrews Hall. Its chapel was gloomy and poverty-stricken. Of the six windows five were 'bumbled' and one dirty. On the left of the room red curtains hung from a rough wooden arch in front of a small harmonium. There were only about a dozen chairs.

The actual ceremony was splendid enough. There were banners studded with gems. A priest in a cloth-of-gold cope. Two acolytes in scarlet cassocks. Huge candles. Incense. A body of choristers. Father Ignatius spoke a great

deal about 'the deficiency of church-services in Norwich
. . . and the vice and immorality in the city'. He said it was
the mission of himself and his brethren to save the citizens'
sinful souls.

What the citizens thought of the Monastery was soon
evident. 'Much curiosity still continues to be exhibited
whenever any of the brethren appear in public,' the *Bury and
Norwich Post* told its readers on 8th March. The little boys
jeered at the monks' sandalled feet and legs, red with cold,
all the more incongruous as the weather was currently very
wet and the streets in a filthy state. On Sundays a great
number of street boys congregated outside the Monastery,
whistling, cat-calling, and making other hideous noises, to
the annoyance of the peaceable inhabitants.

On Palm Sunday there was a huge mob 'of low mechanics and boys' gathered outside the Monastery before eight
o'clock in the hope of tormenting the monks as they went in
procession to St. Gregory's church. Three monks only
emerged to be met with all sorts of abuse.

A full-scale procession did leave the Monastery on
Easter Sunday with a choir of boys singing hymns and the
National Anthem as they walked along. As this took place
before six o'clock on Easter morning it did not help to
endear the monks to the local residents.

By this time stories were circulating about 'miracles' that
had happened in the Monastery. Father Ignatius had put out
a fire by making the sign of the Cross. The wooden head of
Christ on the crucifix had been seen to turn. Despite Lyne's
'bad press' he was making many converts. The Reverend E.
A. Hillyard of St. Lawrence's Church was one of them. He
was to sacrifice much for Father Ignatius. He began by
opening his church to the brethren when they had been
barred from St. Gregory's. What this entailed can be seen
from the report in the *Post* on 5th April 1864:

'As usual on Sunday morning, a large congregation of

'outsiders' assembled at St. Lawrence's Church. This place
of worship being now patronized by the 'brethren'. . . . the
Rev. E. C. Hillyard was the officiating priest, Ignatius
presiding as usual at the organ. The majority of the audience
was very young and easily impressionable. So great was the
pressure of the crowd when the monks were expected to
come out, that a message was despatched to the station for
an officer. Surprise has been expressed at the Bishop not
interfering to prevent these scenes in St. Lawrence's
Church . . .'

The above reference to a 'young and impressionable'
audience was soon to become an accusation that the Monastery was seducing youngsters from the religion of their
parents or relatives. Lay people who attended the Monastery services were given the name of *The Third Order*. One
of the *The Third Order* was an orphan-lad who lived with
guardians and had expectations of much wealth. To their
horror he had declared his intention of becoming one
of Ignatius's monks and giving all his property to the
Monastery.

There was trouble inside the Monastery too. As early as
April 1864 Father Ignatius had placed an advertisement in
the *Church Times* warning readers about two of his monks
who had absconded with their habits, which belonged to
the Monastery, and might beg for alms on the pretext of
collecting for their Norwich brethren. Throughout his
residence in Norwich, Lyne was frequently absent on
preaching tours and whenever this happened the Monastery
seems to have fallen into disarray. The culmination came in
June 1865 when the place was taken over by rebel monks
and a new 'Abbot' installed briefly in Lyne's place. This was
all symptomatic of the lack of organization which was to
end in financial disaster for all concerned in 1866.

If his success was to be measured by the number of his
converts Father Ignatius must have been well pleased. *The*

St Lawrence's Church. A redundant church now standing in St Benedict's Street, which in the 1860s was known
as Upper Westwick Street. It is built in the Perpendicular
style and has a tower 112 foot high.

Third Order was so numerous that admission to the Chapel, by now greatly enlarged, had to be by ticket only. Unfortunately the same extravagant behaviour that had resulted in his earlier expulsion from a Scottish parish began to manifest itself again. Infuriated that members of his *Third Order* had attended a dance in St. Andrew's Hall he made them do medieval penance. The women had to lie prostrate in ashes on the floor of the Monastery chapel, and the men had to be publicly caned on the altar steps. This finally alienated the devoted Reverend Hillyard and St. Lawrence's Church was thereafter closed to the 'brethren'.

Then there was the question of the little boy, named by Lyne 'The Infant Samuel'. He had more or less adopted this child because his mother was unable to bring him up. He had him clothed in a monk's white habit, employed a woman to care for him, and kept him by his side when he preached. This was frowned upon by many.

Father Ignatius might eventually have weathered the various storms of hostility. By 1865 the newspapers had lost interest in him, apart from an occasional snide comment. But with every month that passed this unworldly man's financial position worsened. Had he been a rogue he would have been living on the fat of the land. He was not. He was a visionary and quite impractical. He spent money he did not have on extensions to the chapel. The Elm Hill Monastery was not his. The Reverend Drury of Claydon had raised the money for it. Yet when Drury repossessed the Monastery in May 1866 (Lyne had gone to his parents' home to escape his debtors) Lyne hotly resented it. He fought to get it back, quite unreasonably, for another ten years.

In the *East Anglian Handbook* for 1877 is the following report:

'On June 18 1876 Father Ignatius was expelled by force from the building that he had erected, and the right to which he said he had not made over . . . Some two or three days

before the 18th, [he] gained access to the building, and held
various services in it, there being, as usual, large attend-
ances. On the 18th Mr. Clabburn, solicitor, and a couple of
bailiffs went to the building . . . Ignatius refused to leave
and told the men of law that if they reached the altar, it
should only be over his dead body . . . Allowed half-an-
hour to clear out, he persistently refused to leave . . . The
bailiffs had therefore to carry him out.'

That was not the end, though. Not quite.

'Before he left Norwich, he held some spirit-stirring
services in the city, and that at St. Andrew's Hall on the
Sunday evening will long be remembered by the thousands
who were present, for the address delivered was certainly of
a most powerful and eloquent character.'

The Flood

Winter came early to Norfolk in 1878. In early November snow lay three inches deep in the streets of Norwich after a severe blizzard. A hard, but short-lived frost followed. Then came rain. And a thaw. Then more rain. On Monday 11th November people were saying they had never seen the Wensum so high. Their voices were not agitated. No-one seems to have had a thought of incipient danger. The water remained high all week. On Saturday morning rumours began flying around the city. The trains to Norwich had been stopped at Brundall because of flooding. Bridges had been swept away. The mail cart had been lost with its driver at Saxlingham. Within hours these stories had all been proved false. The Norwich folk shook their heads in disgust. These country-folk! What scaremongers they were! All this fuss about a river.

Certainly the Wensum had risen visibly that morning. It was particularly noticeable in that stretch which has Heigham Street on its south bank and St. Martin-at-Oak on its north. Still, there was nothing to worry about, or so apparently thought the fathers and mothers who set off on their usual shopping expeditions that Saturday afternoon. Many housewives were probably still clearing away the dinner-dishes when the first water slopped over the river banks and into the streets. The flooding was first noticeable at two o'clock, then all at once a miniature tidal wave came rolling along the Wensum's course. Broader than the river it surged as far as St. Margaret's on the south bank, and St. Martin-at-Oak on the north. It rushed into the courts and alleys, invading the ground floors, sending the terrified residents screaming upstairs. They leaned out of their windows, yelling for help.

Assistance arrived with amazing swiftness. Men appeared, as if from nowhere with boats and ladders, and horses and carts. Crowds huddled at the edge of the flood, cheering vociferously when each rescue was effected. Some of the volunteers put their own lives at risk as they manoeuvred their craft through the narrow passages.

By Saturday evening the situation had worsened. The water was roaring through St. Miles Bridge just a few feet below. Houses near the bridge had been flooded. So had a large part of the Anchor Brewery. Between St. Miles' Church and St. Martin-at-Oak, stretched what looked like a lake. In the churchyard of St. Mary's the tombstones were just visible above the water. People stood at the end of St. Swithin's Terrace and listened in terror to the roar of the water as it thundered along Lower Westwick Street. New Mills Yard was impassable. What if the Mills gave way? This was the City Pumping Station. If that collapsed, it would be like a dam bursting.

The flood now stretched along Barn Road as far as Lothian Street. Unaware, an anxious woman opened her door to see if her husband was coming. The torrent rushed in. She just managed to grab her children and carry them upstairs, where she leaned from the window screaming for help. Hers was only one of many miraculous escapes.

Inevitably there were the tough old birds whom not even a flood could dislodge. They said they would rather be drowned than leave their homes. So they had to be left. For those who had been plucked from the waters, and for

St Michaels at Coslany as drawn by James Sillett, 1828.
Built c. 1500, this church, also known as St. Miles, is
renowned for its flintwork. Redundant, it is now a
Martial Arts Centre.

their rescuers, the public houses remained open all night.

On Sunday morning the waters were still rising. The Mayor, Harry Bullard, called a meeting at the Guidhall. Soon handbills appeared in the flooded districts advertising, 'Coffee, Tea, and Bread for all Persons in Distress through the present Floods'. These were being served at eight different centres, mainly schools. The Governor's House at the City Gaol was to be warmed and made available for homeless people.

A few individuals showed outstanding initiative. One of these was The Reverend Mr. Caldwell, Vicar of St. Martin's. On Sunday morning he first rowed along to his church to inspect the damage, then he set about organizing a bread-supply for those of his parishioners who were still marooned. He had a batch of bread freshly baked. He then somehow acquired a 'catamaran' boat in which he could enter the narrow passages of the yards. With a larger boat, containing the bread, to accompany him, he went on his rounds. On his instructions, the grateful recipients let down long pieces of string or rope from their windows. The loaves, thus secured, were then hoisted up.

On Sunday afternoon the sightseers arrived. 'Thousands upon thousands' according to the *Argus*. What was there to see? Flooded factories. Burst sewers. The river at St. George's Bridge 'simply terrible to look upon'. Water flowing through the windows of the *Mercury* office. The Quay completely covered. Bishop's Bridge unapproachable. The King Street yards under water. The Carrow Works damaged. All these to be gaped at, perhaps photographed, certainly stored in the memory to be described no doubt to grandchildren in another century.

There was a public meeting at the Guildhall that evening. People were told how and where they could receive help. The Bishop was providing food and clothing at the Palace. The Dean and Chapter were offering soup. Twenty beds were available at the Boys' Home. The Drill Hall would be open to victims and blankets would be supplied. Blankets, coals and kindling, were being taken round to those who were marooned.

I don't suppose anyone was in a mood to see the humour in the Mayor's regretting the absence of Mr. Chamberlin 'because he had got soaked'. Or in the City Engineer's statement that he had advised the people to remain in their houses above the New Mills, but that many persons had left them without reason. The only danger was at the Mills for should they fall numberless houses would certainly be swept away. But as the water was equally balanced on either side of the Mills, 'the danger was not so great'!

Mr. Stevenson, a member of the committee, who had been to the gaol, complained that many people were going there just to see what the inside of a gaol was like!

It was clear, by now, that the water was going down. Much relief was expressed. At least conditions would not worsen. That Sunday night accommodation was found for about 800 people, no mean feat.

On Monday there was a noonday meeting at the Guildhall to open a Fund for the victims. A subscription-list was started there and then, and within minutes £2000 had been donated. Mr. Savage, a butcher of St. Andrew's, gave forty stones of beef. Bush & Company sent a barrel of their biscuits. Bullards supplied whatever brandy was needed.

By Tuesday the waters had greatly receded. Now began the unpleasant and onerous task of clearing up and trying to make good the damage. Thousands of dead rats lay in the mud. A number of live ones were huddled together on the half-submerged barrels in Bullard's yard. Astoundingly there had been only three human victims of the disaster, all men, one only seventeen years old.

The damage done to property had been considerable. In Heigham countless homes of working-folk, who had toiled

St Mary at Coslany. Dating mainly from the second half of the 15th century, this aisle-less church has an earlier Anglo-Saxon round tower, and a fine two-storeyed porch. It is currently a Craft Centre.

for years to buy their possessions, had been destroyed. The *Argus* reported 'chairs and tables fallen to pieces, carpets covered with filth and salt . . . pianofortes and harmoniums irretrievably ruined, (while) outside the houses, the gardens and pretty greenhouses have been utterly demolished, heaps of fowls and rabbits lie about, killed by the water, favourite dogs have been drowned, and lots of canaries have died (from lack of drinking-water) in the upper stories.'

In St. Miles', St. Martin's, and St. Mary's, the yards had been wretched places even before the flood. Now they were abominable. In this district many small shopkeepers were facing ruin. Not only had they lost their stock. Their many 'credit' customers who paid their dues on a Saturday night had not been able to do so. Nor would they ever. For, according to one shopkeeper, 'you must nail them when they have the chips'.

On the whole the 'humbler classes' had behaved pretty well, the Relief Committee agreed. The one blatant case of roguery had come from a gentleman 'of a class above the poor'. This blackguard had claimed compensation for a gold watch which he said he had lost on Sunday, while carrying people from their homes, . But, according to the police, he had reported the watch missing twelve hours before the flood started. 'Name him!' the horrified assembly demanded. Mr. Councillor Field, who had reported the case, refused to sink so low. The one crumb of comfort which he was able to hand out was that the villain, so he hoped and believed, was not a Conservative!

In the end the Fund amounted to well over £5000, which was a considerable sum of money in 1878. The citizens seemed to feel that the disaster had been coped with not only adequately, but very well. Doubtless many of them echoed the fervent prayer of the *Argus* chronicler: 'May Heaven prevent the necessity of ever having to make such an Appeal again!'

Chapel Field Gardens

The main attractions in Chapel Field Gardens are probably the pavement chessboard and the fascinating Gurney Clock, whose futuristic-looking casing is designed to show off its unique eighteenth-century Harrison Regulator. The latter is a comparatively recent acquisition, presented to the city by Barclays Bank (formerly Gurney's) to mark their two hundred years in Norwich.

If the Gurney Clock has changed the appearance of the gardens, it is not the first time that has been altered. These eight acres have undergone many vicissitudes over the centuries, a lot in the name of progress. To begin with there was just farmland. It belonged to a college of priests known as St. Mary in the Fields, or the Chapel in the Fields. This institution was founded in the mid 13th Century and stood where the Assembly House stands today. By the time of the Dissolution, the Prior of Buckenham and the Prioress of Carrow also owned part of the land. When the fields were handed over to the City fathers, after 1548, they turned it from arable into pasture land and leased it out to private individuals.

By 1578 the Chapel Fields were used as an exercise ground for the militia of both city and county. The trained bands were mustered here annually between 'Bartholomew tide' and Michaelmas. The area had been officially designated as 'a meet and fit place to charge guns with shot and powder for the exercise of shooting in hand guns, etc.,'. This function was to be retained throughout subsequent centuries. In 1668, according to the Chamberlain's accounts, the City tent was erected 'in Chapley Field' for the use of the Deputy Lieutenants during the General Muster. It was set up again in 1671 for the Lord Lieutenant of Norfolk and Norwich and his deputies, who were to hold a general review of the City Regiment.

That the area had more pacifist, and equally necessary functions we know from a complaint made by the Mayor and Court to Lady Hobart, who was the lessee in 1656. Contrary to her lease the lady was allowing stiles, ditches, and 'tenters' to obstruct the Fields, to the hindrance of citizens. 'Tenters' are the frames on which lengths of wet cloth are dried and stretched after they have undergone that stage of cloth-making which is known as 'fulling'. In the 17th century 'tenter-yards' were normally adjacent to the premises of the clothiers.

It was the middle of the 18th Century before the 'Fields' moved in the direction of the public park. By then the ground had been railed in. Thomas Churchman, whose handsome house still stands in Bethel Street, was the lessee, and he planted trees and created three broad walks for the convenience of the inhabitants. It is thought that he also used part of the Fields as an extension to his own private grounds.

In 1792 Chapel Field underwent a complete transformation both in appearance and in use. It was leased by the proprietors of the waterworks for a reservoir. The construction of the reservoir which was 300 yards in circumference and encircled by a deep trench, must have created not only a stir locally but plenty of jobs as well. It remained in use until 1852 and was enjoyed as a skating rink in those winters when it was completely frozen over. No doubt

The Drill Hall. Designed by J. S. Benest, it opened on October 31, 1866. In its heyday it performed many functions apart from a military one. It survived two wars, but not the age of the motor-car.

many Victorians sighed regretfully when the new reservoirs were opened at Lakenham, and the Chapel Field was drained and filled in.

The Victorian Militia and Volunteers were still drilling and being reviewed like their Elizabethan forefathers. In 1866 a grand building was erected on land which had been leased to the City Rifle Volunteer Battalion. This was the Volunteer Drill Hall, which was officially opened by the Prince and Princess of Wales. Norwich was very pleased with this hall which stood in the north-west corner of the field. In the guide-books of the early 1900s it was still being proudly described as 'a pleasing imitation of an old English castellated building'. One of the towers of the City Wall was incorporated into the structure, which housed an armoury, and a residence for the drill-instructor. The Drill Hall was in frequent use as an exhibition-centre and conference-hall. In 1868 it was the venue for the inaugural address of Dr. Hooker, the President of the British Association for the Advancement of Science. The Prince of Wales attended Freemasonry conventions here in his capacity as Grand Master of the Lodge. It was used to house bazaars and displays, and before the Agricultural Hall was built, the renowned Christmas Shows of the Fat Cattle Association. Perhaps its finest hour came in the Spring of 1881 when the great National Fisheries Exhibition was held in it. On this occasion it had to be extended and it was illuminated for the first time by electric light.

While the Drill Hall was an object of pride to Norwich's respectable Victorians, the Chapel Field itself was the opposite. They did not care for the spectacle of pipe-smoking labourers lounging on the rough grass during their meal-breaks. Nor for the labourers' children who played rough and noisy games there. They frowned on the Evangelical preachers who disturbed the Sabbath tranquillity with their raucous meetings. Moreover the 'Field' was claimed to be the evening resort of 'disreputable persons'. In 1877 it was decided that it had to be put in order. By 1880 it had been transformed into a civilised park with flower-beds, a children's playground railed off beside the Drill Hall and, the pièce de résistance, a magnificent ornamental pavilion, which had been exhibited by the firm of Barnard and Bishop at the United States Centenary Exhibition in Philadelphia in 1876.

The original cost of the Pavilion had been £2000, but it had been sold to the city for a modest £500, which had been raised by public subscription. It was two-storeyed, with a spiral staircase, ornate carving and a pagoda-roof covered with curved tiles of zinc. Its main function was as a bandstand and although the park still has its bandstand, the exotic pagoda was demolished in 1949.

By the end of the 19th Century the 'Chapel Field' had become 'genteel'. Access was by four gates, which were closed at sunset on the ringing of a bell. There were walks, broad and narrow, lined with seats. There were beds of flowers and shrubs, fountains and avenues of trees. The Police Band played in the pavilion.

In 1841 Grigor, the Scottish horticulturalist, had written in his 'Eastern Arboretum', 'Chapel Field, from its being so much the resort of loose and idle boys, and being occupied partly by washer-women, seems to be in a great measure deserted by the respectable citizen.' This was the case no longer.

When the Lights Went Out

Few people in Norwich were expecting war during the summer of 1914. The mood of the city was optimistic. Trade was looking up. The weather was fine. The assassination of the Austrian Archduke and his wife on 28th June was shocking. But it had happened in a remote country called Serbia. How could it possibly affect the lives of ordinary people who were listening to the band in Chapel Field Gardens or enjoying a spending-spree 'down the market'?

Within five weeks they had learned their mistake. The assassination had been a lighted match applied to a strategically-laid fuse. Austria had declared war on Serbia. Germany, having declared war on Russia, was now threatening France and Belgium. The whole of Europe was rising in arms. Could Britain remain on the sideline? On 3rd August, Bank Holiday Monday, a crowd stood all day in front of the *Eastern Daily Press* offices waiting for news. Tuesday found Norwich a subdued and worried city. That night, just before twelve o'clock, a special edition of the *Eastern Evening News* came out. It told its readers that Great Britain and Germany were now at war.

In Norwich, as in other towns and cities, a Local Emergency Committee was set up. Its members had quickly to decide what steps to take in the event of an invasion. They started by drawing up a list of all cars and motor-cycles owned by Norwich residents. The Mayor then made an appeal for cars that might be used by the army in an emergency. Two hundred cars and about the same number of motor-cycles were made available by public-spirited owners. Three hundred owners volunteered to drive their vehicles for the army when they were needed. The committee then listed the remaining private cars within the city boundaries. These were grouped according to locality and a motor-mechanic, who had to be sworn in as a Special Constable, was allotted to each group. These mechanics were to 'disable' all the cars in their sector if the enemy invaded. Motor-cycle owners were sent instructions on 'disabling' their own machines.

In 1914 the second main form of transport was still the horse, or the horse and cart. The responsibility for this was handed over to a Civilians' Emergency Corps. Twelve hundred men who were used to working with horses were enrolled. In the event of an invasion, these men were to arrange for the horses and carts in their various sectors to go to an agreed meeting-point for dispersal among the military. If conditions made this impossible they were to shoot the horses and disable the carts.

Another scheme which the Emergency Committee adopted was suggested by the Norwich Division of the British Medical Association. This involved earmarking certain city schools for dressing-stations in the event of an enemy air-attack. The city's doctors were told which schools they must go to if they received word that enemy aircraft were approaching. Casualties would be transported to the nearest 'dressing-station' school by the Red Cross.

For some reason it was thought that refugees, as many as fifty thousand at a time, might well come flooding into Norwich. A vast stock of cocoa was laid in. A central depot was earmarked for the reception of the refugees, and

various public buildings were designated as overnight
shelters. The Committee even had cards printed with the
name of a specific shelter at the top and a space beneath in
which the refugee was to write his/her name and address.

Happily none of the above schemes ever had to be put
into operation. Had an invasion ever occurred there was a
body of fighting men ready to defend the city with their last
drop of blood. The Volunteer Training Corps, the 1914
equivalent of the Home Guard, went on parade for the first
time on 15th December. It comprised 600 men over the age
of thirty-eight and men who, for some reason, were not
eligible to serve in the Territorials. Three times a week the
various squads drilled in their different halls in the city. On
Thursdays and Saturdays there were afternoon drills on
Earlham Road Recreation Ground. Men from all ranks of
life joined the Corps, many of them elderly. Sadly they
were not held in very high esteem, being referred to locally
as 'England's Last Hope'. By 1915 they had changed their
name to the City of Norwich Volunteers and were looking
much more professional. Now they had cycling, ambu-
lance, and signal sections, and on Sundays they assembled
in the market place before going on route-marches. Towards the end of 1915 they, and other Norfolk Volunteer
companies, worked at the construction of the airship station
at Pulham. They supplied men to patrol vital stretches of
railway-line during the hours of darkness. They had training exercises and fought large-scale mock 'battles'. In fact
they ended by projecting much the same image as that of
their successors in World War II.

The war was into its third month before the threat of
air-raids began to be taken seriously in Norwich. Officialdom suddenly realized that a brightly-lit city would be a
wonderful target for a raiding Zeppelin. In November 1914
it was politely suggested to the shopkeepers of Norwich
that the lights in front of their shops might constitute a

Inspection of the Volunteers. These conscientious gentlemen drilled two or three nights a week and were ready to die to defend their city. But apart from a red armlet, they had to supply all their own equipment and their uniforms.

danger. Very few took any notice. At the beginning of December the public were instructed to light only essential lamps from then on and to shade them in some way. After darkness the lighted tramcars now travelled with drawn blinds.

The city was still considered to be too light and bright for safety. Now requests became orders. All lights outside shops had to be shaded black and red. No light could be used that was visible from the outside of any building. Street-lighting was reduced to a minimum. By this time Lynn and Yarmouth had suffered air-raids, so the 'black-out' orders were willingly carried out by most residents.

As air-raids over the Eastern Counties became more frequent Norwich's 'black-out' regulations became more and more stringent. No street-lighting at all was permitted. Evening-classes, evening-meetings of organizations, and evening church-services were all discontinued. Shops and factories closed early. Householders learned how to darken their windows completely, using edgings of black, sticky tape. Car headlights were shaded. Cyclists made their perilous way along the black streets with the aid of candle-lanterns hooked over the front lamp-brackets of their cycles. The newspapers regularly contained amusing anecdotes about people mistakenly walking into the houses of strangers, or colliding with trees, gateposts or lamp-standards. Stories circulated about highly-strung ladies who screamed 'blue murder' if they heard a footstep behind them in the blackness. Some Norwich citizens took to wearing luminous discs on their fronts in the hope of avoiding accidents. Not unnaturally the people began to grumble. It was felt by many that the precautions had been taken to a ridiculous length. But the authorities were adamant. They said that blacked-out Norwich was an example to the rest of the country. And perhaps they were right.

After all Norwich did not suffer a single Zeppelin raid in the four years of war.

There were other ways in which the war was to alter the lives of the people of Norwich. The workers in one shoe-factory which had specialized in satin and brocade dress-shoes, soon found themselves making French Army boots and brogues for the Scottish Highland regiments. Several factories began to produce Cossack boots for the Russian army. Machinists in the clothing-factories were now sewing up khaki uniforms instead of dress-suits and evening-dresses. And the goods they were turning out at the Leather Works were now designed to stand up to the mud and water of the trenches.

What was going on across the Channel was soon brought home to the people of Norwich as the first tragic convoy of wounded soldiers arrived in Thorpe Station on 17th October 1914. One hundred of them were transported in Red Cross ambulances to the Norfolk and Norwich Hospital. The Thorpe War Hospital was opened to accommodate a large number of wounded and various small hospitals sprang up around the city. They were never to lack for patients. The 'killing-fields' of France and Flanders produced a mighty crop.

Too often Norwich men, who had set off for the battle-fields full of patriotic fervour, never returned. Wives became widows. Fatherless children abounded. Some were helped by grants from the Royal Patriotic Fund. Doubtless they were assured by someone 'high up' that their men had not died in vain, that by his sacrifice he had helped to win 'the war to end all wars'.

'Who shall forget the day of the Armistice?' a local author, Percy Izzard, wrote. 'That sunny morning the multitude thronged at a word to the heart of Norwich and filled it with their shoutings and their songs. A bloom of flags innumerable broke in all the streets, on all the towers.

St. Peter's epic peal sent the message out in stirring changes, and in the crowd there were those of pensive face who could find no speech, who hardly could listen to the bells with dry eyes. Overhead, the airmen from Mousehold tumbled like plover at their games; below, sedate folk joined with those of high spirits in extravagances of joy. And many went into the churches to give solemn thanks'.

That night the lights went on again.

Return of the 2nd Norfolks. They had had a vile war,
fighting the Turks in Mesopotamia. The terrible climate
and terrain of the desert, and diseases like beri-beri and
typhus had taken their toll of their comrades.

Theatrical Festivities

In 1951 Norwich was chosen as one of the principal centres in which the Festival of Britain was to be celebrated. Determined to show that the honour had been deservedly bestowed the civic authorities thought long and hard about the form of the celebration which would take place between 18th–30th June. They had in mind a particularly splendid Festival of the Arts akin to the Triennial Musical Festivals for which the city had long been renowned. After reflection they decided that the area of this Festival must be extended. In common with the rest of Britain, Norwich was celebrating its survival and recovery from World War II. In the course of that war, 340 of its civilian citizens had been killed in air-raids, over 1000 had been injured, and many of its sons and daughters had died fighting for their country. These people came from all walks of life, and their interests were equally varied. So Norwich's 1951 Festival was ultimately designed, as far as was possible, to represent them all. It was officially opened on Sunday 17th June with a special service in the cathedral.

There were three grand street processions which took as their theme, 'Norwich Through The Ages'. Queen Elizabeth I and her train of courtiers rode through bomb-scarred streets where patches of wasteland were still being reclaimed. Horned Viking warriors sat in their longship borne along on the back of a sturdy lorry. The organizers saw the processions as the counterparts of the medieval guild-pageants, hopefully involving the majority of the citizens either as participants or spectators.

The central concert hall for the duration of the Festival was the original Odeon cinema in Botolph Street, a building which was pulled down in 1969 when the present Odeon was built as part of the Anglia Square complex. It had seats for 2000 and although its amenities were regarded as being of luxury standard an attempt was made to keep the ticket-prices within the range of ordinary members of the public. The opening concert on 18th June was given by Sir Thomas Beecham and the Royal Philharmonic Orchestra. On the following Wednesday there was a piano recital by Dame Myra Hess, who had done so much during the war to boost morale with her London lunch-time concerts. On the evening of Saturday 23rd June the London Symphony Orchestra, under the conductorship of John Hollingsworth, played 'Music from the Ballet'. This feast of classical music was extended into the following week when the Triennial Musical Festival was held concurrently with the Festival of Britain. This brought more great names to the city, Sir Malcolm Sargent, the pianists, Clifford Curzon and Eileen Joyce, and the violinist Max Rostal.

Popular events were interspersed among the classical concerts. On 19th June the well-known ventriloquist Peter Brough and his 'doll' Archie Andrews entertained audiences at the Odeon. On Friday the 22nd, Tom Jenkins was there with his Palm Court Orchestra, and on the 24th, Geraldo and his Concert Orchestra headed the bill of a variety concert. These entertainers all had wide audiences through their radio programmes so were regarded as top attractions.

There were three 'live' theatres in the city in 1951, the major one being the Theatre Royal in Theatre Street. It was the third building to stand on the site. The second, a Wilkins building dating from 1826, had been tragically destroyed by fire on 22nd June 1934 and it was thanks only to the proprietor Mr. Jack Gladwin that a third Theatre Royal rose from the ashes to open on 30th September 1935. Fortunately this building survived intact through the 1942 air-raids which did such damage in St. Stephen's and in Rampant Horse Street. It is one of the most prestigious provincial theatres in the country, its reputation having been on the ascendant since its acquisition by the City Council in 1966.

In 1951 the Theatre Royal provided Norwich audiences with a varied programme mainly from visiting theatre companies. Plays, musical comedies, light opera, and ballet, with the customary Christmas pantomime, made up the year's programme. Typical perhaps of their audience's taste was the choice of production for the first week of the Festival: Gilbert and Sullivan's *HMS Pinafore* and *Trial by Jury*, both performed by the Norfolk and Norwich Amateur Operatic Society.

The Maddermarket Theatre, although much smaller than the Theatre Royal, was a marvellous asset to any Festival whose theme was the celebration of national history and culture. It was the creation of Nugent Monck, then seventy-three years of age, a man of remarkable talent and vision. Nugent Monck had originally come to Norwich in 1908 at the request of Mrs. Colman to produce a series of historical tableaux in St. Andrew's. Hall. Apparently while looking for somewhere to store his furniture he had chanced upon a dilapitated property in Ninham's Court which runs between Chapelfield North and Bethel Street. This house, lovingly restored, became his home and acquired the name of 'The Crypt'. He remained here until his death in 1958.

Monck's work with amateur actors in the city began in the years before the First War. The group which he had gathered together established their first permanent theatre in the Music House in King Street in 1914. With less than a hundred seats the audience was small and select and the Music House productions were aimed at the erudite and the connoisseur. The fare of medieval Mysteries, translations from the Greek dramatists, Japanese 'Noh' plays, and the occasional Shakespearian production, is said to have appealed to the clergy from the not-too-distant Close.

In 1921 Monck realized his ambition of acquiring larger premises for his company, now known as the Norwich Players. Down in the Maddermarket was a Georgian building which had been at various times, a Roman Catholic church, a Salvation Army hall and a baking-powder factory. Monck transformed it into an Elizabethan theatre with gallery and apron stage, in fact the kind of theatre for which Shakespeare's plays had originally been written. His dream, now realized, was to have the plays performed as Shakespeare had intended. He had abundant support. Periods of working at the Abbey Theatre, Dublin, had brought friendship with such literary giants as W. B. Yeats and George Bernard Shaw. Eric Linklater, John Masefield, and Gwen John were also enthusiastic supporters of the enterprise.

That the civic authorities had envisaged the Maddermarket's playing an important rôle in the 1951 Festival can be seen in the words of an Appeal launched by the Lord Mayor, Alfred Baines, in 1949: 'The city of Norwich,' he wrote, 'owes much of its distinction in the artistic sense in this generation to the theatre which Mr. Nugent Monck has directed so brilliantly for over twenty-five years past. Now at seventy-one years of age, he is very anxious to secure the theatre's future, and he has most generously offered to give all the tangible assets of the theatre to a new trust, representative of the Norwich Players, the citizens of Norwich, and the patrons of the drama in general . . . To extend the seating of the theatre by 100 seats will probably cost

The Maddermarket Theatre by T. Stead, c. 1921. Standing in a paved courtyard off St John's Alley, the Maddermarket Theatre has retained its policy of having amateur players under a professional producer. Its Christmas productions are a delight.

£15,000 . . . An endowment fund of £10,000 is needed in addition to guarantee that a new director can make adequate use of the riches of Mr. Monck's gift, which represents all his savings and the fruits of his life's work. If the enlargement of the theatre is to be completed in time for the Maddermarket worthily to play its proper part in the Festival of Britain in Norwich in 1951, the raising of the funds is a matter of urgency.' One of the more unusual features of Maddermarket productions was that the amateur players invariably remained anonymous. For the Festival they gave performances of *Pericles* and *The Taming of the Shrew*.

The Hippodrome theatre, which stood in St. Giles, where now there is a soulless multi-storey car-park, was Norwich's music-hall. The building had originally opened on 3rd August 1903 as the Grand Opera House but by the end of 1904 both the name and the entertainment offered had changed. The re-christened 'Hippodrome' provided vaudeville entertainment for the man-in-the-street, two houses nightly and a change of programme every week. From 1930–37 it changed its spots yet again, and in deference to the taste of the day, became a picture-house. It returned to being a live variety theatre in time to entertain wartime audiences, and in 1942 it was hit by a bomb which sadly killed the stage manager and his wife, and two of the performers. In 1960 it finally closed despite attempts to rescue it by locals who cherished fond memories of the place. In 1951, however, it was still providing the city with variety programmes in the tradition of the old English music-hall, and this was its rôle during the Festival fortnight.

For those who preferred their entertainment to be out of doors, there were bowls-drives, tennis tournaments, and brass bands playing most evenings in Eaton and Waterloo Parks. There was dancing in Chapelfield Gardens every evening from nine o'clock until midnight, and from ten p.m. until one a.m. the city was illuminated. It must have been a heartening interlude for a city which was still licking its war-wounds, and suffering from post-war austerity.

Industrial Norwich

The 1951 Festival of Britain celebrations included an Industrial Exhibition in St. Andrews and Blackfriars Halls to commemorate Norwich's past, demonstrating a justified pride in the present state of its trades and businesses, and looking hopefully towards the future. It was a purely local affair, and it is interesting, and sometimes sad, to see what has become of those firms who advertised themselves so proudly in the Festival guide-book.

In 1951 the footwear industry provided the city's main source of employment, with one-fifth of Norwich's workforce being distributed around the various shoe-factories. James Smith, the founder of Southall & Co., (manufacturers of the famous Start-Rite shoes) is regarded as being the father of the whole of the city's shoe industry. In the 1790s he had a shop at the back of the market on the site where the present City Hall stands and it was while running this business that he had the innovative idea of producing ready-made shoes on a standard last rather than made-to-measure shoes. As the industry grew over the next century, shoe factories sprang up, but until the end of the nineteenth century, much of the work was 'out-work', done by workers in their own homes. Gradually machines were introduced and the factory system took over, the industry taking a great leap forward after the First War, when women's skirts were shortened for the first time and there was a new demand for fashionable ladies' shoes. By 1951 there were around 5,000,000 pairs of boots and shoes being produced annually in the city, most of them for women and children.

Amongst the firms advertising in the Festival guide-book were the Norvic Shoe Company, founded in 1856, and claiming to be, 'the largest producers of women's shoes in Britain'; Sexton Son and Everard of St. Mary's Works; James Southall & Co. Ltd., of Crome Road; Edwards and Holmes, Ltd., 'designers and makers of fine shoes for ladies'; Bally of Norwich; Van-Dal Shoes of Salhouse Road specializing in 'promenade and evening shoes'; Barfield and Richardson, makers of the 'Boofers' range of women's casuals; and Shorten and Armes Ltd., of Esdelle Street, manufacturers of 'Fiesta' evening sandals for ladies. In recent years cheap imported shoes have stolen the market from our own high-quality footwear. We can see the consequences of this today in the buildings which once housed the Norvic Shoe Company and Sexton Son and Everard respectively. Both firms are now defunct. The grandiose former factories are being remodelled to accommodate offices and shops.

One branch of the textile industry which was still going strong in the city in 1951 was the manufacture of Norwich silk. At their factories in St. Mary's and Mile Cross, Francis Hinde & Sons, Ltd., produced crêpe de chines, georgettes, satins, chiffons, and taffetas with a high international reputation. Visitors to the Festival could be taken on guided tours of the mills if they so desired. How many of them would have believed that within thirty years the mills would be no more? Hinde's were taken over by Courtaulds in 1964 and finally closed as uneconomic in 1980. Today not even the building remains to remind us of those past glories.

The engineering industry was well represented in the

Festival exhibition. Barnards, agricultural engineers and ironfounders, could boast that their founder, Charles Barnard had in the 1840s designed the first loom in the world to produce wire-netting, (a loom that can be seen in the Bridewell Museum today). By 1871 the factory, then known as Barnard, Bishop and Barnard, covered a large area in St. Michael's, Coslany, and was producing a wide variety of articles, from wire-netting to slow combustion stoves and mangles. Because of the nature of their products, the firm flourished during both World Wars. In the Second War their Mousehold factory had the unhappy distinction of being the target of some of the first bombs to be dropped on the city in July 1940. Happily Barnards still survives as part of Tinsley Wire Industries of Sheffield, and has large premises on Salhouse Road, Norwich where various kinds of wire fencing are produced, some of them highly specialized.

Boulton and Paul's was another local success story that could be told with pride at the 1951 Festival. Originating at the end of the eighteenth century in the ironmongery business of William Moore, they had gradually expanded by skilfully adapting to the requirements of different generations. Thus at the turn of the century they specialized in all kinds of glasshouses and conservatories. During the First War they began building aeroplanes, and they eventually crowned their achievements in that line by constructing the metal frame of the R101 airship. During the Second War their contribution both to the armed forces and to civil defence was considerable. Consequently they became a prime target whenever Norwich was bombed. In 1951 they appeared to be thriving with a variety of subsidiary companies under their umbrella. Few people can have envisaged that by 1987 all their busy Norwich workshops would be closed, leaving only the firm's Head Office to keep the name alive in the city of its birth.

Messrs Bullard and Sons Anchor Brewery, late 19th century. The brewery was built on a site near St Miles' Bridge at the beginning of Queen Victoria's reign and

remained there until 1966, when brewing ceased. The
buildings were gradually demolished and today blocks of
flats stand in their place.

The firm which could claim to have the largest single works in the city in 1951 was not an engineering concern, but a manufacturer of foodstuffs. Colman's, makers of the world-renowned mustard, and of cornflour, semolina, and starch, had a river frontage of well over half a mile on a fifty acre site at Carrow. Two thousand workers were employed by this firm which had been started early in the nineteenth century through the initiative of Jeremiah Colman who owned the water-mill at Stoke Holy Cross, four miles from the city. He saw the potential of manufacturing mustard, first for national consumption, and later for export. It was his great-nephew, another Jeremiah, who, in 1856, had mills built in Norwich itself for the manufacture of mustard, flour and starch.

The first Jeremiah Colman was a non-conformist and a philanthropist, much loved in the city, of which he was Mayor in 1846–7. His successors – notably Sir Jeremiah Colman Bt (1859–1942) – devotedly carried on the tradition of service to Norwich both in the holding of civil offices, in social work, and in charitable gifts and benefactions. The Colman Local History Library, the Colman Gallery in the Castle Museum, and Suckling House on St Andrew's Plain are three of the splendid gifts made to the city by this remarkable family.

Colman's today is well-known for its range of baby-foods and soft drinks as well as its original products. In 1973 to mark the firm's 150th birthday, they opened the delight-ful Mustard Shop in Bridewell Alley. This is fitted out like an early nineteenth century grocer's shop with a small mustard museum.

A. & J. Caley Ltd., was another food-and-drink manu-facturer exhibiting at the Festival. Their advertisement in the guide-book was composed of photographs of the mod-ern staff facilities in their newly-built factory at Chapel-Field. The original A. J. Caley had had a chemist's shop in

London Street, where in 1863, he started the manufacture of mineral waters in his cellar. By the early 1880s, the business, by then a family concern, had moved to Chapel-Field. At this point the firm decided to branch out in other directions. Mineral water manufacture peaked in the summer, but during the rest of year the demand was small. It was decided to manufacture first cocoa, and as a result of that, chocolate. The link between chocolate-manufacture and the making of festive crackers, the firm's next venture, may not at first glance be evident. It was simply to provide further employment for the women and girls who made the boxes and paper frills for the chocolates.

In 1932 the firm was taken over by the large concern of John Mackintosh & Sons, and it remained thriving until 1942 when virtually the whole factory was destroyed in an air-raid. Rebuilding started after the war and it was photographs of these large new premises that were so proudly displayed in 1951. The mineral-water side of the business was moved to another new factory under the control of a local brewery, and Caley's Crackers Ltd moved to the industrial estate on Salhouse Road. (It is now Tom Smith's & Co. Ltd.) Another amalgamation in the chocolate-producing world in 1968 produced the Rowntree Mackintosh combine which owned the Chapelfield factory until 1988. It was taken over then by the Swiss Nestlé group with a workforce of 1000, compared to the 2000 workers employed there in 1951.

The Festival guide-book classed the city's four main breweries as among the smaller but still important industries. They were all long-established and their premises were familiar and well-loved landmarks to many Norwich citizens. The home of two of them Morgans, and Youngs Crawshay and Youngs, was in King Street. Bullards' great Anchor Brewery was at St. Miles Bridge, and Steward and Patteson's Pockthorpe Brewery was off Barrack Street, (their trademark was a print of the old Pockthorpe City Gate, which had been demolished in 1792, the year before the brewery was established.) Sadly today brewing is no longer one of Norwich's main industries. In the 1950s a battle of attrition began. Ten years after the Festival of Britain, both Morgans, and Youngs, Crawshay and Youngs had gone. Bullards had bought the former, and had combined with Steward and Patteson's to buy the second King Street brewery. In a few years they in turn were taken over by the giant, Watney-Mann. Houses and flats now occupy the sites of the magnificent Anchor and Pockthorpe Breweries where names like Brewers Court are reminders of a traditional local industry.

Printing was another of the smaller but important local industries represented at the exhibition. The largest firm, Jarrolds, employed 850 workers in 1951 and printed and bound several million books annually. They were already engaged in the valuable pioneering work in colour photography and illustration printing which has earned them international fame. Theirs was another success story to be proud of. Their founder, John Jarrold, had opened a print shop, on the site of Jarrolds' present London Street shop, in 1823. By the end of the century this had become a four-storey building comprising printing-works and shops. Most important, for those who worked for the family, was their paternalistic attitude to their employees, which as in the case of the Colmans, continued from generation to generation.

As Norwich looks towards the year 2000, the gaps left by those industries which have disappeared, are happily filled again. Many people work in electronics and electrical engineering. There are firms making chemicals, plastics, windows, and refrigeration equipment. We live in a different world from that of 1951. And Norwich has had to adapt. She has done so sensitively. Even a few hours in her company reassures us on that point. This is the same 'fine old city' which George Borrow so admired and loved.

Bibliography

Norwich Trade Directories 1783–

Norwich Mercury, Bury and Norwich Post, Eastern Daily
   Press: 18th C–

Blomefield, F. (1805–10): *Essay towards a Topographical
                    History of the County of Norfolk.
                    Vols. 3–4*

Mason, R. H. (1884): *The History of Norfolk*

Victoria County History of Norfolk (1901–6)

Green, B. and Young, R. (1981): *Norwich: The Growth of a
                    City*

Wade-Martins, S. (1984): *A History of Norfolk*

Barringer, J. C. ed. (1984): *Norwich in the 19th Century*

Chapter 2: *The Life, Letters and Sermons of Bishop Herbert de
          Losinga.* ed. Goulburn and Symonds (1878)

Chapter 5: *The Paston Letters.* ed. Gairdner (1910)

Chapter 8: *The Letters of Sir Thomas Browne.* ed. Keynes
          (1931)

Chapter 9: *An Account of the Sufferings of the People called
          Quakers.* Besse, J. (1753)

Chapter 10: *Letters of Humphrey Prideaux to John Ellis.* ed.
           Thompson (1875)

Chapter 11: *An Account of the Scots Society Etc.* Norwich
           (1784)

Chapter 13: *The Norwich School of Painting.* Rajnai, M.
(1978)

Index of Names

Acknowledgements

The extracts from *John Bilby's Journal* (MC 27/2) and from the records of the Society of Friends (SF/various) are by permission of Norfolk and Norwich Record Office.

Norman Scarfe has kindly allowed me to quote from *A Frenchman's Year in Suffolk, 1784*. La Rochefoucauld. (Ed. Scarfe).

Norwich Museums Service supplied, and gave permission to reproduce plates on pages 35, 48, 67, 73, 91, 119, 128, 170.

Pages 135 and 176 are reproduced by permission of the Norfolk and Norwich Local Studies Library.